The Mom-to-Mom Guide to the Baby Years:

Reviews, Ratings and Recommendations From the Trenches

Stephanie Gallagher, Editor

Design by Peri Poloni. Knockout Books
Copy Editors: Josephine Rossi, Karen Sultan, Susan Benovitz

ISBN 0-9720667-1-3

Table of Contents

Introduction

This book was going to be called *Everything We Know About Babies We Learned in Nordstrom's Bathroom*. If you haven't had the privilege of experiencing the ladies room at Nordstrom first hand, you are missing one of the most heavenly delights of being a mom with a baby.

For starters, they have comfy cozy couches all over the place, where you can relax, rest a bit, and feed your baby in peace and quiet. Since the "mother's room" is separate from the regular bathroom area, nursing moms can breastfeed in semi-privacy, as the only other people there are moms with little ones, many of whom are nursing, too. And they have the most wonderful changing tables! Big, thick padded tables – long enough and wide enough to accommodate big babies and toddlers, with a waste slot for diapers right underneath and a sink to wash your hands just a step away.

But the best part about Nordstrom's bathroom is the moms. You can meet tons of 'em there, swap war stories about labor and delivery, share tips on coaxing a burp out of a gassy baby, and relay tricks for getting baby to sleep through the night. You can learn the secrets of buying designer baby clothes at rock-bottom prices and compare the relative merits of organic versus regular baby food. It's the kind of "tribal wisdom" that can only be learned from other moms — or your own experience.

Of course, most of us don't sit around the bathrooms of department stores hoping to glean child rearing advice. We gather these precious pearls on the parks and playgrounds of our neighborhoods. Or we take a Mommy and Me or Gymboree® class. All of which are great ways to connect with other moms. But they aren't the most efficient ways to gather intelligence, and they still limit your findings to a small circle of women. In *The Mom-to-Mom Guide to the Baby Years*, we bring all of this wonderful wisdom together in one place. It's like having a huge gabfest with more than 140 moms from all over the world.

Indeed, 142 moms contributed to *The Mom-to-Mom Guide to the Baby Years*, to be exact. And we did so in the spirit of helping other moms learn from our experience, achievements and mistakes. We are moms just like you – breastfeeders and bottle-feeders, vegetarians and meat-eaters, working moms and stay-at-homers. We live in the city and the country, on military bases and in suburban neighborhoods. We are financially comfortable, and we are penny-pinchers, deaf and hearing. We come from Rapid City, South Dakota and Murfreesboro, TN, Ontario, Canada and Kyoto, Japan. But what we all share is a desire to do the best we can in raising happy, healthy children.

We know that being a mom isn't easy. Even the 20 of us who have been through medical school concur that it is the hardest job we've ever had. Indeed, it's a little like boot camp in that you don't know what to expect or how to cope until you go through it.

But it shouldn't have to be that way. You should be able to get all the wisdom, shortcuts, secrets and tricks that moms have passed down from generation to generation in one easily-accessible place. And that's precisely why we created *The Mom-to-Mom Guide to the Baby Years.*

What you won't find in this book are objectively-tested product comparisons, verified on 62 points of durability, design and function in a government-certified test lab. But you will find advice on the relative merits of car seat/stroller travel systems versus lightweight stroller frames. And it'll come from moms who've had to haul the things in and out of their cars while holding their breath, so they don't wake their sleeping babies.

You won't be able to compare the features and prices of six different high chairs side by side, but you'll discover which is the only one worth the money – and where to find a terrific and inexpensive alternative that does just as good a job. And you won't get a board-certified physician's prescription for the proper way to administer medicine to a child who refuses to take it. But you will get tricks from moms — including doctor moms — who've had to struggle with the same challenge and have discovered innovative ways to do the job.

The truth is our homes, cars, playgrounds and parks are the most rigorous testing labs in the world, and that's where our advice has been invented, tested and proven to work.

The Mom-to-Mom Guide to the Baby Years is the first book to take the product reviews, time-saving secrets and mom-savvy shortcuts that have been learned in the trenches, and put them on paper – all in one place for easy reference. We hope you enjoy this treasury of tips and tricks and that you'll share with us your comments and suggestions for future editions. Write to survey@soundbitepress.com with your ideas. We look forward to hearing from you.

CHAPTER 1:

Pregnancy

Oh, the aches and pains of it all! We may love the idea of growing a child, but pregnancy also means morning sickness, weight gain, stretch marks, leg cramps and an inability to go more than 20 minutes without peeing (okay, not really, but it feels like that).

The worst part about going through it the first time is that you don't know what to expect. Then when you go through it again, you're a veteran, except you discover that every pregnancy is different (if you didn't have morning sickness the first time, you could have it for nine months the second), and that your body doesn't bounce back nearly as fast as it did the first time. Here is our best wisdom for handling the most common pregnancy challenges.

The Five Best Remedies for Morning Sickness

1. Crackers, especially Saltines and especially when eaten first thing in the morning
2. Ginger anything – ginger ale, ginger tea, ginger snaps
3. Lemon anything – lemon drops, lemonade, lemon verbena oil, lemons
4. Eat small, frequent meals.
5. Eat protein.

WHY WE RECOMMEND THEM

"Keep crackers on your night table so you can grab one or two the minute you wake up. It gets something in your tummy and staves off the nausea for a short time. Second, ginger anything! Ginger snaps, ginger ale, anything with ginger in it is a great morning sickness remedy. Ginger is calming to an upset tummy."

–KAREN HURST

"One of the many books I read when I was trying to conceive mentioned that lemons, lemon drops and lemon oil can be helpful in taming nausea. I purchased lemon verbena oil (an essential oil you can get at any health

food store) the weekend I found out I was pregnant. It smells like very concentrated lemons. I would just crack the top on the vial of oil and sniff any time I felt sick. Ninety-nine percent of the time, my stomach would calm right down. It worked wonders."

–COLLEEN GRACE WEAVER

"I always tried to make sure I had something in my stomach. It helped to munch on crackers, bread, etc. and to drink lots of water."

–STEPHANIE ZARA

"Lemons, lemonade and lemon drops all worked really well for me. Anything sour in taste helped with the nausea."

–WENDY DOUGLAS

"I'm on an email loop of moms, and one of the ladies suggested ginger. Anything with a bit of ginger works. I liked ginger snaps because they put a little something in my stomach, and that helps morning sickness also. But you can get ginger candy and gum also. It's the best kept secret."

–BRENDA BROWN

"Eat something (like a cracker or two) BEFORE getting out of bed (have someone bring it to you, or leave it on your night stand the night before). It always seemed easier to avoid nausea by eating little amounts frequently than to stop nausea once it starts."

–CHELSEA COFFEY HAMMAN

"I had horrible morning sickness until about week 18. I craved protein and bought a Burger King egg and cheese bagel or croissant almost every morning. The sandwiches tasted great and I didn't have to smell the eggs cooking."

–KIMBERLY MERCURIO, M.D.

Your Essential Maternity Wardrobe

About three months into this pregnancy gig, the morning sickness wears off (well, that's the way it's supposed to work, anyway). Then you get a short grace period before you begin to realize that NOTHING IN YOUR CLOSET FITS YOU ANYMORE. What to do? Veteran moms know that being comfortable is key. Regardless of the season, you'll need a basic wardrobe that will take you from work to play to evening in comfort.

TIPS FROM THE TRENCHES

✓ **Stay with styles you normally wear.**

"First, I would recommend that you stick with the type of clothes you wear normally — don't buy floral, feminine clothes if your style is tailored, etc. Pick one color and build your wardrobe around that. Black works well for winter and for working wardrobes. Also, buy a couple of outfits that the top and bottom come as a matched set for the days you are just too tired, sick, etc. to even think about getting dressed.

—CLAIRE BIENVENU

✓ **Buy classic clothes in natural fabrics.**

"I plan on having lots of kids, so I expect to be pregnant quite a bit in the next few years. When I bought maternity clothes, I kept this in mind and bought classic styles that wouldn't go out of style over the years. Then I added a few pieces with that year's fashion. Plus, I bought higher-quality stuff so that it would last. The most important thing is comfort, and as pregnant women sweat quite a bit, natural fibers are essential since they 'breathe.' Cotton and linen are best."

—CARA VINCENS

✓ **You may want clothes that don't hug your stomach, as some women get very sensitive on their tummies when pregnant.**

"Baby doll dresses work best. There are times when you just don't want anything touching your tummy, and even if it has the elastic maternity panel in front, it still irritates you."

—K. SCARLETT SHAW

"Those pants with the stretch panels were a definite no-no for me. The seam where the panel was connected to the non-stretch fabric always cut into my belly. I got one of those wardrobe-in-a-box sets that was great, came with a short skirt, leggings, a jumper dress and two shirts (short sleeve and long sleeve). Comfy and stylish!"

—MICHELE LONGENBACH

THE FIVE MOST IMPORTANT PIECES EVERY PREGNANT WOMAN NEEDS IN HER CLOSET

1. Stretch pants or leggings, preferably in black, for the winter
2. Bike shorts for summer
3. Comfortable shoes
4. A good supportive bra and comfortable underwear
5. One nice outfit you can wear for special occasions, holidays and nice dinners out

WHY WE RECOMMEND THESE

"I recommend simple pieces, such as black leggings or slacks, jeans and a simple white maternity top. But more importantly, I would really suggest a comfortable, but attractive pair of slip-on loafers. Your feet really do swell up, and tying shoes can get to be challenging when you're in the last trimester. I always suggest a nice simple dress...the maternity version of the little black dress can take you from dinner out to office parties to showers easily."

–MEGAN MARTIN

"Stretch pants, lots of tees and for summer, cute bib overall shorts were the best – and cotton sun dresses with the spaghetti straps. I still felt sexy and comfortable."

–ELAINE AUTRY

"I loved being pregnant and wanted the world to know, so I loved wearing the obvious 'maternity clothes' look. However, the most important items in my pregnant wardrobe were hardly ever seen. The real essentials included a super-comfortable, front-latch, all-cotton (if you can find it) sleeping bra! Your ever-growing breasts can be painful, especially at night as you toss and turn. A good sleeping bra (similar to an exercise or jogging bra) can keep your breasts supported and lessen the discomfort.

"Comfortable panties are another must, and I found gigantic briefs to do the trick, as long as they were big enough to go completely over the belly. Anything hitting the waistline was torture. After my pregnancy, I was told by friends that they liked bikinis for the same reason (they didn't restrict the waistline).

"Whether or not you are one of the women whose feet swell in pregnancy, near the end of the pregnancy, you will find bending over to be less than fun. Bending over to tie your shoes will be downright

annoying. Take care of your comfort and sanity by having comfortable slip-on shoes or sandals that you can manage to slip in and out of without help."

–THERESA SMEAD

"Buy some basic black capris (or pants, if winter) to go with a variety of tops. This really stretches your wardrobe."

–JENNIFER YOUNG

"I recommend maternity underwear. It is so much more forgiving than regular underwear, and they do have different types."

–DIANNA SCHISSER

"First, black pants. I worked in an office and I would wear those pants every day. No one ever noticed! They were so comfortable and went with everything. Second, comfy, slip-on shoes. I gave up trying to tie my shoes somewhere around the sixth month. Third, supportive bras. I knew I was pregnant when my chest exploded. Supportive bras are the best investment."

–SARA HAMMONTREE

"I recommend Lands' End leggings. You can buy them in normal sizes. I got the Tall sizing – it gives you more length from crotch to waistband. I also got a Large. Believe it or not, they stretched to accommodate me in my ninth month, and they were supportive immediately postpartum, too."

–SARAH PLETCHER

"I resisted buying maternity underwear with my first pregnancy, [but later when I tried them], I couldn't believe how much more comfortable (although ugly) they were."

–TAMMY MCCLUSKEY, M.D.

"If you're working, it is way easier to stick to the basics, black and white. A shirt here or there that has some color in it would be good to add flair. Take as many clothes as people are willing to lend you. The variety in styles and sizes will be handy later on."

–STEPHANIE R. SMITH

OUR FAVORITE HEALTHY PREGNANCY SNACKS

1. Fruit...by itself, with cottage cheese, in a shake or smoothie

2. Peanut butter and...crackers, whole wheat bread, celery, carrots, banana, jelly, pretzels, apples, bagels
3. Yogurt
4. Raw vegetables with dip or in salads and sandwiches

WHAT WE LOVE ABOUT THEM

"Strawberries, bananas, vanilla pudding and milk in the blender is a fantastic breakfast on the run or late-night snack...and helps you get the fruits and calcium that seem hard to get enough of."

–REBECCA CURTIS

"I craved spinach salads, topped with grape tomatoes, feta cheese and blue cheese dressing. Lots of calcium, which may help with pre-term labor, good amount of calories, and it's not too heavy to eat through those days of nausea."

–TRACI BRAGG, M.D.

"I had chocolate organic yogurt. It really helped me make it through pregnancy without caffeine and still stay awake at work."

–BETH BLECHERMAN

"Prunes. I ate a ton of the lemon- and orange-flavored ones. Not only do they have a lot of iron, but they help alleviate constipation."

–SARA HAMMONTREE

"I ate a lot of veggie roll-ups with cream cheese, spinach leaves, roasted red peppers, shredded carrots and scallions on a tortilla. When I wanted more protein, I added slices of chicken."

–PATRICIA ARNOLD

"I liked frozen green grapes."

–CHANTAL LAURIN

"I liked yogurt with granola mixed in and raw veggies. I didn't really eat any more than when I wasn't pregnant, so I had to make sure the food I was getting was good food. I would bring raw veggies with dip into work and keep them on my desk for easy snacking."

–GENEVIEVE MOLLOY

"I would always eat apples with peanut butter."

–ANGELA ALBRIGHT

"I lived on peanut butter. It gave me the extra protein I needed for my twins. I made a sandwich and wrapped it, and I kept it at my bedside for those hungry times in the middle of the night."

–LORI VANCE

THE BEST ADVICE WE GOT WHEN WE WERE PREGNANT

If you haven't gotten enough advice from your doctor, your mother or your spouse so far, don't worry. By the time you enter your seventh month, you'll have gotten more advice than you can stand from every one of your friends who's ever had a baby. And your relatives, too. Oh – and let's not forget your neighbors. And then there's the cashier at the supermarket – she'll probably regale you with the story of her entire 42-hour labor as she scans your Häagen Daz™.

There's just something about pregnancy that brings out the, well, maternal in all of us. It's a little like living through a war in that the only people who really know what it's like are the ones who've been there. Unfortunately (or fortunately, depending on how you look at it), when it comes to motherhood, half the population (or so it seems) has been there, and they are all too eager to tell you just how to do it right. The good news is a lot of this advice can be helpful, especially when it's given in the spirit of generosity. Here's what we mommies felt helped us the most.

TIPS FROM THE TRENCHES

✓ **Rest.**

"Get plenty of rest, because once the baby's here, sleep can become a thing of the past!"

–JENNIFER CLEVELAND

"Rest as much as possible. I tend to overdo it at all times, and during my first pregnancy I ended up exhausted. Not with my second!"

–LAURENCE THELLIER

"Take it easy, relax, get rest and go swimming when possible. The swimming was great because it made me feel so light, and it took all the pressure off my joints. I could just float and relax."

–MARI KISTLER

✓ Use this as an opportunity to really take care of yourself and do what you like doing.

"Just take advantage of pampering yourself any way you can. When you're pregnant, there's so much you can't do (hot tubs, hot baths, soft cheese, sushi, alcohol, vigorous or risky exercises like skiing, etc.) that you have to take advantage of the things that will make you feel good about being pregnant – indulge in snacks you can eat (buy prepared meals from a gourmet grocery, for example), get a pregnancy massage, take naps, buy fun maternity outfits, take time for yourself and get a lot of sleep!"

–STACEY SKLAR

"Go see lots of movies while you can still be out with your husband for long periods of time without a babysitter."

–KARI RYDELL

"Take care of you during this time. You will be taking care of others for the rest of your life. So get a pedicure, a massage, have your hair done, have your cards read, whatever makes you feel good."

–DANA A. CROY

✓ Relax and enjoy it.

"Relax and let nature take its course. When you are very big and pregnant, all you want is for it to be over. It was helpful for someone to remind me what a great time it really is."

–BROOKE KUHNS

✓ Don't take everyone's advice seriously. Listen to what makes sense and forget the rest.

"The best advice I received was, 'Don't take anybody's advice.' Use what you can and dump the rest! It seems that when you are pregnant, everybody has advice for you…men, women, people that never had kids, people that wanted but couldn't have kids, people that were pregnant but miscarried, people that knew people that had kids, people that had

BIZARRE pregnancies and people that had kids. This advice relieves the guilt of not using all of the advice given!"

–GENEVIEVE MOLLOY

"Everyone and their grandmother thinks they have some jewel of wisdom that you just have to know. And not only do you have to know about it, you are expected to use it too. But if you ever sat down to go over all of that unsolicited advice, it all contradicts itself."

–DANIELLE MARION-DOYLE

✓ Let go of your perfectionism.

"The best advice I got was not to be a martyr. In the end, no one cares whether your bathrooms were cleaned once a week or twice a week or whether each shirt was folded perfectly. It is more important to relax and enjoy the pregnancy and take care of yourself, so the end result is a healthy baby. This was the best advice because it came from my husband who was the one who had to put up with the messy house (and yes, he pitched in and helped too!)."

–RIVKA STEIN, M.D.

✓ Put your own happiness – and your relationship with your partner – first.

"Remember that you are a couple first, and parents second, because when parents take time for each other, they are happier, and a happy loving family is the core for happy children."

–SABRINA LANE

✓ Take it as it comes.

"Don't go into labor with a bunch of expectations. For example, don't think that 'I'm not going to get an epidural,' or 'I definitely want an epidural.' I think that birthing plans are good things, just anticipate being flexible. Otherwise you may be setting yourself up for disappointment. I went in without any expectation and ended up being quite happy with my birthing experience."

–CHELSEA COFFEY HAMMAN

CHAPTER 2:

Delivery and Beyond

If this is your first baby, you may be concerned about labor and delivery. We aren't going to go into all the wonderful, icky, messy, painful and downright weird things that MIGHT happen during your delivery. That's what prepared childbirth classes and The Learning Channel are for.

Instead, we focus on what to bring to the hospital, how to handle the first few weeks and months at home, the importance of keeping yourself and your own needs front and center and that ever-annoying, though all-consuming (pun intended), subject of losing the pregnancy weight.

What to Bring to the Hospital

Books and prenatal childbirth classes are famous for coming up with long lists of items to bring to the hospital. We found some of these suggestions to be helpful, but many of these items never got used. Here's what we think are the critical items to pack in your hospital bag.

THE TEN MOST IMPORTANT THINGS TO BRING TO THE HOSPITAL WHEN YOU'RE READY TO DELIVER

1. Camera and film
2. Robe
3. Nightgown or pajamas with easy access to your breasts, if nursing
4. Phone numbers of everyone you know
5. Socks or slippers
6. Pads
7. Car Seat
8. Pillow from home

9. Snacks

10. The baby's father!

WHY WE RECOMMEND THESE

"Bring a camera/video to capture the moment, a list of phone numbers to call family and friends and a pretty nightgown/robe so you feel a little bit presentable for visitors."

–JENNIFER YOUNG

"A robe is really important to cover yourself up when company arrives. And lots of pads! The ones they give you are horrible. And a phone book with all the names and phone numbers you could possibly need. Example: Your other kids' school number, the numbers of friends who are helping to take care of your other children, the pediatrician's office number, etc."

–ANDREA SUISSA

"I recommend a camera and film, your pillow from home (make sure your pillow case is brightly-colored so the hospital staff doesn't think it's theirs), your favorite soap, shampoo, etc. It will feel so good to take a shower with these after you give birth."

–REBECCA ALDER

"I recommend bringing the biggest hospital-size pads you can find and lots of large underwear. I remember that they gave me pads with belts (like from the '50s!) that were not too comfortable. The other two things would be a good comfortable robe that is not too expensive (so you don't worry if it gets dirty) and some really comfortable slippers."

–BETH BLECHERMAN

"A robe. Those hospital gowns show more than you want people to see. Your baby's baby book – hospitals will put baby's first prints in that section of the book if requested. Also, you can have them autograph it. And bring plenty of film. It's amazing how many of us later realize we didn't take enough pictures of our baby's day in the hospital."

–BOBBI ANNAL

"Clothes, a camera, and make-up. It's amazing what a little makeup can do to make you feel like you didn't just go through 12 hours of labor!"

–TESSICA BEZENEK

"Your own pajamas and slippers (those hospital floors are cold!) for the day after you deliver so you can feel a bit less institutional from the traditional hospital garb. Now that I am having my third, I might bring my own pillow to be a bit more comfy in those lovely hospital beds."

–ANN STOWE

"One, hard candy to suck on during labor. Two, a car seat. I actually forgot this one! And three, extra special snacks and such for after delivery. Sometimes they are slow with the food or the food isn't good or filling. These helped me stay more alert."

–BECKY GASTON

"A camera, some nightgowns for the baby with the hand covers since not all hospitals have T-shirts with the little hand covers to prevent the baby from scratching his or her face, and your baby book if it has a page for baby's first footprints."

–REBECCA HARPER

"Besides your husband?! A nursing bra, PJ's and/or robe and relaxation tapes. Oh, make-up, too, since EVERYONE on the planet will come to visit."

–SHERYL MADDEN

"A button-up nightgown (if nursing), phone book, to-dos for the extra quiet time, a mommy memory book (now is the time it's all fresh in your mind) and announcements."

–ELAINE AUTRY

"A massage therapist. Really, it was the absolute best thing for me during my labor. She was a lifesaver."

–CHANTAL LAURIN

Coming Home

Those first weeks and months after having a baby are filled with emotion – abundant love for this sweet little newborn combined with hair-pulling exhaustion and often, bouts of depression. Many of us focus exclusively on the baby's needs, often to the detriment of our own. Paradoxically, however, the best thing you can do – for the baby as well as for yourself – is to put your needs front and center. Here are our best ideas for making your transition to life with a new baby easier

TIPS FROM THE TRENCHES

✓ **Do whatever you need to do to limit visitors in the first few weeks, especially those who expect to be treated as guests.**

"Stay in your bathrobe or nightgown when people come over. It will keep them from staying too long. Stay in bed and rest that first week especially."

—AMELIA STINSON-WESLEY

"Repeat after me, 'My doctor recommends I have as few visitors as possible in the first two weeks.'"

—DONNICA L. MOORE, M.D.

"I did not answer the phone much in the first few weeks, but I did put a baby update on the answering machine every couple of days just to let people know that we appreciated their calls. I gave a brief idea of what the baby was doing and how we were handling it."

—TAMARA PRINCE

"DO NOT entertain the people who come to help with the baby. Make certain they are there to help you, not be guests, and not to take over the baby. You need the time to get to know your baby — to nurse when the baby needs to nurse, so you can get in sync with each other."

—KATE HALLBERG

"Limit visits from family and friends. Don't feel guilty about saying no if someone wants to come."

—DENINE SCALLEN

✓ **Get help.**

"I think that getting help when you have a newborn is key. It is so exhausting and isolating to be at home with a baby, and if you never get a break, it's really hard. Find someone to do the laundry, pick up groceries, make meals, and watch the baby for an hour or two. Even if you just go to your bedroom and read or watch TV, it'll be worth a lot."

—SHARON LICHTENFELD

"Give the new dad plenty of responsibility in caring for your baby. While you may feel possessive now, the time will come when you will want and need the help, and if dad doesn't learn how to help now, he won't be equipped when you really need him later. Plus, you want your baby to have the strongest possible bond with dad, and this is how it starts."

–THERESA SMEAD

"If people offer to cook dinner or clean, let them. This is one time in your life that people are going to offer to help, so don't pass it up, even if you are normally an independent person. No one can prepare you for how tiring it is to take care of a newborn."

–BRANDY CHARLES

"When people offer to help, let them. Don't worry about the world outside of your new family. Sleep when the baby sleeps. Don't worry about getting stuff done – it doesn't matter."

–JAMIE HUNLEY

"I have one important suggestion: BABY NURSE, BABY NURSE, BABY NURSE. We did it on our own, and it was exhausting, even though we had great support from our families. The baby nurse can cover the night shift (help the mom recover by getting some sleep) and assist with getting the baby on a good sleep/eating schedule."

–BETH BLECHERMAN

"Take the help offered. Order out. Have a maid service once a week or every other week for at least the first four months."

–ELAINE AUTRY

✓ Make sleep a top priority. Get rest in whatever way you can, as often as you can.

"First, I would recommend having the hospital nursery keep the baby at night while you are there. I am nursing, so the baby was brought to me during the night when needed for feedings, but otherwise, was cared for at night by the nursery nurses."

–CLAIRE BIENVENU

"Rest whenever the baby rests. Sometimes I would try to get a lot of things done, catch up while the baby was sleeping. Then I would be tired. I should have listened to that advice more."

–SHANNON GUAY

"The best thing that happened was my mother-in-law came over once a week and stayed the night with me. I had bottles of breast milk pumped in advance and she would care for the baby during the nighttime until I woke up in the mornings. This was so wonderful because I knew that if she needed me, all she had to do was knock on the door, but I also knew that I did not have the responsibility for the night. It's amazing what one night of good rest can do for you."

–BRANDY CHARLES

✓ Take care of your body.

"Get plenty of rest, eat healthy and drink tons of water. Also, take long, warm baths to ease the pain, use cabbage leaves (sparingly) to relieve engorgement and also be sure to wash your hair and take a shower. It's amazing how much better you feel after a shower. Also, don't forget to continue doing your Kegel exercises to help you heal faster!"

–ANNA MARIA JOHNSON

✓ Take the pain medicine.

"I know there will be a lot of flack from this, but take the drugs. If your doctor prescribes you medication after your birth, take them! Why be a hero? They help with pain, relaxation, and I never had sore nipples from breastfeeding. Make sure your doctor knows you are breastfeeding and writes the prescription accordingly."

–TIFFANY ZIMMER

✓ Let the house go.

"Adjust your expectations of housework; don't worry about what is or isn't clean. If you didn't have time to prepare meals in advance, order take out and have someone go get it."

–AMELIA STINSON-WESLEY

"It took me awhile to realize that my house would not implode if I didn't clean it every day. A new mom has to realize that the mess will still be there later. When the baby rests, so should you (although, I still can't manage to do that.) Take time for a shower, even if it means that you don't get a load of laundry done that day. I found that 20 minutes by myself in the bathroom would change my attitude for the whole day."

–SARA HAMMONTREE

✓ **Prepare meals and stock up on household supplies in advance.**

"Stock up on staples, canned goods, paper goods, diapering supplies and household items to get you through the first month. Make sure you have everything you need so you won't have to worry. Stock your freezer with meals, frozen veggies, etc., so you can just pull something out instead of cooking."

–CLAIRE BIENVENU

"Accept offers of meals or make up frozen casseroles in advance of your due date, so you can pull them out and heat them up. Usually, dinner time is the most fussy time for babies, and it's difficult to try to prepare a meal when you're dead tired and have a crying baby to deal with."

–JULIE BARTLETT

✓ **Do something nice for yourself every day.**

"Try to shower every day. It makes you feel more human. Even try blow-drying your hair one of the days in that first week – something to make you feel like 'you' again. Drink plenty of water and try to laugh as much as you can."

–KATE STEIMAN

"Ask for a spa treatment or massage for your baby shower, and make sure to get at least an hour to yourself everyday."

–NINA McCANN

Your Wardrobe After the Baby is Born

When you're pregnant for the first time, you often fantasize about getting back into your regular clothes after the baby is born. But once you've had one child, you know those skinny jeans don't just glide on moments after giving birth. Here's what we recommend you have on hand for those first few months after the baby comes.

TIPS FROM THE TRENCHES

✓ **Comfort is key.**

"For me, all three times after delivery, the skin on my belly was very sensitive the first week after delivery, and the most comfortable clothes were loose-fitting clothes, like dresses and very stretchy underwear."

–BARBARA NICHOLS

"I found that buying pants with Lycra™ (stretch) is good for when you want to start wearing real clothes, but you are not yet down to your pre-pregnancy weight. Lands' End has washable stretch pants that work great. My favorite pants with stretch are the Halogen and Classiques Entier brands at Nordstrom. They have high waists and stretch to make the fit comfortable, but look good. They are great for when you are first pregnant and after the baby when you have not quite returned to your pre-pregnancy weight. And they last, which is important."

–BETH BLECHERMAN

"Be realistic. Keep out the maternity clothes and some larger, loose-fitting clothes – anything that is comfortable."

–HEATHER HENDRICKSON

"I would say a good pair of yoga pants are a MUST. Old Navy sells them and they are SO comfortable and look cute with anything from T-shirts to sweaters."

–BETH MILLER

"Japanese Weekend [brand] 'before and after' pants are great as your body wilts, sags and shrinks. I also had some baggy pants with elastic that were nice. Buy one of each style of nursing bra. Just don't overload yourself on one of any style; then once you know what you like, buy a dozen."

–KATE HALLBERG

✓ Get tops that allow easy access to your breasts if you're nursing.

"I think nursing gowns are for the birds, same with the shirts. They don't work very well. Snap-up shirts are the best for nursing because they are easy to get out of in a hurry (and believe me, you hurry when you have a screaming, hungry baby on your hands!). Next best are T-shirts – big ones. I still wear my maternity T-shirts because they give me the room to pull them up and feed the baby."

–HEATHER MEININGER

✓ **Realize that it took you nine months to get to your top pregnancy weight; allow yourself nine months to get back down to your normal size.**

"Don't be fooled into thinking you will be back to your pre-pregnancy weight right after you give birth. Don't feel guilty or bad that you have to wear maternity clothes for a while after. It's better to be comfortable in these than miserable trying to squish yourself into your favorite jeans. It took me eight months before I could get into my jeans and another month before they looked good."

–CARA VINCENS

✓ **We differ on whether or not to keep maternity clothes. Some of us note that you'll be living in them for the first few months after giving birth; others say get rid of them immediately in order to force yourself to get back in shape. You decide which approach is right for you.**

"It was so discouraging to look at any maternity clothes after my daughter was born. I bought a few shirts and pants that were four sizes bigger than normal. I loved being able to wear jeans again. Besides, as I started to lose weight, it felt good to shrink out of those things!"

–SUSAN DOBRATZ

Now About Those Extra Pounds...

Once the initial cocooning period has passed – you're getting showers on a regular basis, you get dressed every day (or at least most days) and the aches and pains of delivery have healed – you may be ready to think about how you're going to get back into your pre-pregnancy clothes.

Note: If you got into your skinny jeans two weeks after delivery, please keep that milestone to yourself. We have fragile egos (not to mention wild hormonal mood swings) in these first months after having a baby, and we prefer to not torture ourselves with stories of women whose pregnancy weight melted off them with less effort than a lick of a (nonfat) ice cream cone. Below are the best ways to battle the post-pregnancy bulge and win.

THE FOUR EASIEST WAYS TO LOSE WEIGHT AFTER THE BABY'S BORN

1. Exercise.
2. Breastfeed.
3. Eat right.
4. Give yourself time.

"Without a doubt, jogging is the easiest and fastest way to lose weight after having a baby. You don't have to learn a new skill (you learned that as a toddler!), and you don't have to join a gym."

—ANGELA SNODGRASS

"As soon as your doctor or midwife says it is okay, begin an exercise program. Usually, you can walk shortly after delivery. Walking every day with your baby is a good start. After six weeks, with your doctor's okay, usually you can begin more vigorous exercise, such as running or aerobics. There are many Mommy & Me workout classes available, where you can bring your baby and workout with other new moms. Denise Austin also has a nice pregnancy and post-pregnancy workout tape."

—DIANE BEDROSIAN, M.D.

"I started taking walks with my babies as soon as I felt comfortable doing it. It was nice to get out of the house and spend some time with the baby."

—BROOKE KUHNS

"Getting outside once a day for a walk with the child(ren) is an easy way to get some exercise. Try putting on exercise tapes with peppy music during the day. If you have a toddler, you can encourage them to 'dance' with you. If you have a newborn, they will probably be content to try to focus their eyes on you as you bounce around and listen to the music."

—REBECCA CURTIS

"BREASTFEED and stroll that baby. I was hungrier breastfeeding than I ever was pregnant. I ate almost anything I could and it still wasn't enough. I lost a ton of weight. That also helps your uterus contract, so it makes the belly tighten. I also took lots and lots of long walks in hilly regions. Great workout, and the baby loved it."

—JENNIFER ROSE

"*Breastfeeding! You not only burn more calories, but breastfeeding releases hormones that help your body return to its 'normal' weight faster.*"

–COLLEEN GRACE WEAVER

"*I gained 42 pounds during my pregnancy, and I lost 22 pounds in six weeks without working out. I just nursed my child as often as she desired, and the pounds melted off.*"

–AMELIA STINSON-WESLEY

"*I lost 24 pounds the first week, five the second, and a few pounds each week after birth. I had gained 40, but was down to my pre-pregnancy size six weeks later without doing a thing except breastfeeding (no exercise or dieting at all).*"

–KARI RYDELL

"*Weightwatchers.com. Memorize it. Use it. It works. I was almost into a size 18. (Okay, I was a size 18) and was disgusted. Ellie was 15 months old, and I was 20 pounds away from a size 14 (I'm 6 feet tall). I ran into another doctor mom at the hospital who had clearly recently lost a ton of weight and who looked, well, phenomenal. I asked her what in the world she had done, and how she had found the time. 'Weight Watchers Online,' was her reply. 'It's cheaper [than joining in person], and if you're self-motivated like I am, it works.' Go for it, gals. I've lost it and kept it off for six months now.*"

–MICHELE F. CARLON, M.D.

"*Keep up the healthy diet you had while you were pregnant. If you follow the basic food groups, you will drop the pounds in no time.*"

–LAMIEL OESTERREICHER

"*I do have to say I think my eating habits from the beginning played a big role in losing the weight. Yes, I did eat sweets, but I limited myself. I tried to have a lot of different healthy snacks on hand, so I would eat those, and then I would try to eat healthy dinners. I am no where near being a health nut, but I did try to eat as healthy as possible.*"

–BRANDY CHARLES

"*The best bit of wisdom I heard was, 'Nine months up, nine months down.' Don't try to rush losing weight. If you try too soon, you can jeopardize your milk supply. But don't wait until you are done breastfeeding either. With the additional calories you burn breastfeeding, cutting your calorie intake just a little can make the pounds melt away.*"

–TARA TUCKER

"Just remember that it takes some people longer than others. I had one friend who was back to her pre-pregnancy weight (and skinny!) in two weeks, while it took me nine months."

—KAREN WILSON

"I gained a lot of weight and lost all of it within a year. The only way to do it is to be realistic about how quickly the weight will come off. Give yourself a whole year to be back to normal. But you also really have to exercise. It won't come off by itself. I worked out to a tape and got a ThighMaster."

—SARAH E. CAMPAGNA

"At first I was disappointed about how long it took me to lose my weight. But now, looking back, nine months is not that long. It is really important to stay focused and realize that it's not all going to come off in one day. I work part-time from home, so I have the time to workout every day. This is what helped me the most. I use exercise videos so I can do it while the baby is napping, and I don't need to get a babysitter or bundle him up when it's cold."

—CARA VINCENS

Time for You: Our Best Advice

Just because you've gotten over the hump of those early sleepless nights and dazed days when your baby was a newborn doesn't mean you should go back to trying to be a Superwoman. Motherhood is a marathon, not a sprint, which means you need to take extremely good care of yourself for the long haul. Here's how.

HOW TO HANDLE IT WHEN YOU'RE SICK OF PLAYING PEEK-A-BOO, CAN'T FACE ANOTHER LOAD OF LAUNDRY AND JUST WANT TO ESCAPE

TIPS FROM THE TRENCHES

✓ **Get a change of scenery.**

"Leave the house. Two-fold reason: It calms the baby down just by driving around, and other people always manage to put things into

perspective when they see her in the park or the market and say, 'What a beautiful baby!' I just love to have a conversation with an adult with whom I couldn't agree more."

–MICHELLE GEBHARD, D.O.

"I found that putting the kids in the car for a drive always calms everyone down."

–LAURENCE THELLIER

"Get out of the house. Take a walk around the block, with or without the baby, a trip to the mall where everyone admires your little one, or buy a new pair of shoes. These little things can get your mind away from stress at home."

–TAMARA PRINCE

✓ Do something relaxing – for you and the baby.

"Cuddle up tummy-to-tummy with your baby in a quiet, dim room."

–ELICIA MOORE

"I put my son in his Exersaucer, take the whole thing in the bathroom and take a nice bath with some of his bedtime baby bath!"

–TESSICA BEZENEK

"I think what helps me most is that I go to a gym that has a nursery. My son has been going there since he was two months old and loves it! I go when he is the only child in there. That gives me an hour to exercise and relieve stress. I love it. Then, when he naps, I can shower and relax."

–ANNA MARIA JOHNSON

✓ Do something you enjoy BY YOURSELF.

"I call on someone to take the baby for a little while so I can have some 'me' time. So many mothers forget that you need to take care of yourself as well as the baby. 'Me' time can consist of something as little as taking a nap or shower or maybe getting some much-needed shopping done."

–LAMIEL OESTERREICHER

"My husband watches the baby while I go for a long walk. I listen to books on tape and get exercise at the same time…AWESOME."

–CHANTAL LAURIN

"Babies are God's most precious gift to mothers. Babysitters are the second most precious. Find great babysitters, and hire them as often as you can afford."

–DONNICA L. MOORE, M.D.

"Take a walk, phone a girlfriend, have a glass of wine, treat yourself to something sweet or do your hair and make-up."

–ELAINE AUTRY

✓ **Make taking care of yourself a priority every day, just as you would giving the baby a bath or brushing the kids' teeth.**

"I make sure that I incorporate some 'me' time into every day. The hours of 1 to 3 p.m. are quiet time in my house. All three of my children must either take a nap or play quietly in their room, so that I can unwind after a busy morning and refresh myself for the dinnertime rush. I spend this time doing something that I enjoy like reading a book, taking a nap or chatting with a friend on the phone. This little pick-me-up makes my day run much smoother."

–STEPHANIE MARTIN

"If you don't take care of yourself, you have no energy to take care of anyone else. Think of a car. If you don't do regular maintenance and fill up with gas regularly, it is not of use to anyone."

–DENISE R. GREENWOOD, M.D.

✓ **Connect with friends.**

"Call another mom and hang out together. A little adult company can work wonders."

–ELIZA LO CHIN, M.D.

"Find a local Mothers of Preschoolers or other moms' group. Meet some women who have kids the same age as yours, and plan some play dates. But don't forget to plan some moms-only nights out, too!"

–STEPHANIE HOSSZU

"I read a book or watch a movie (both can be done during feeding times) or get on the computer and talk to other moms."

–WENDY DOUGLAS

"Having a mom and baby group once a week was my savior many times. There was a group of five mommies who all had babies the same age. We would get together once a week and rotate the location. Talking to women going through exactly what you were going through and seeing the babies develop at close to the same rate was amazing. We all looked forward to Tuesdays and hated to miss it. Although a lot of the conversation was about babies, we also shared a lot of talk about husbands, work, meals, swapped recipes, walked and swam together for fitness, and just gave support to one another."

—TAMARA PRINCE

"I went to the hospital to a weekly playgroup. After a short time, I began to form friendships and exchanged phone numbers. Now our playgroup has ten moms and babies. When things are crazy, you can always find a friend to talk, walk or vent to. It is great because the babies are all within six weeks of each other's age, so there are always appropriate tips, advice, stories, etc."

—SUSAN DOBRATZ

"Planning activities with other moms and babies can really help alleviate the boredom and isolation of looking after a baby. I would make socializing a priority above doing the laundry. It makes you feel like you're not alone, it gives you support from people in a similar situation and it keeps your child occupied so you're not the sole form of entertainment. If you don't know many people, there are organized mom and baby groups and activities in most neighborhoods, or just head to the nearest park."

—SHARON LICHTENFELD

✓ Keep perspective.

"Take everything with a sense of humor, because if you can't laugh at what you're doing most of the day, then you are taking things too seriously."

—MARI KISTLER

"Just think about the alternative: Answering to a boss at work, taking complaints from unsatisfied clients and being the 'mature' person with adults who behave like children. Suddenly, the infant is nothing but a ball of charm."

—CAREN SADIKMAN, M.D.

CHAPTER 3:

Equipment: What to Buy

Perhaps the biggest shock to first-time moms (after the realization that your belly will eventually expand to a full 40 inches) is the amount of equipment, gear and just plain "stuff" you need when you have a baby. In this chapter, we share what we've learned about getting the right equipment at the best quality and the lowest price.

Crib

Unless you are planning to co-sleep (i.e., sleep with your baby) all the time, a crib is an essential item and should probably be the first thing you buy. Here's what we look for in a crib.

TIPS FROM THE TRENCHES

✓ **Make safety your number one concern. All new cribs that are sold in the United States should meet current safety regulations. However, many of us have gotten cribs from friends, relatives and garage sales. We do not recommend this; safety standards change all the time, so you really can't be sure that a used crib meets current guidelines.**

✓ **Shop early.**

"By the time my husband and I went to shop for our baby's furniture, we had to pick out something that was displayed on the floor. Everything else would take six weeks to get delivered. It would have been nice to pick out her furniture from a larger selection."

—JODI STEGER

✓ **Look for sturdy construction.**

"It is very important to look for a sturdy build. This is something that a toddler will be thrashing in some day, and you want it to hold up for some time. I would recommend a hard wood, preferably with an easy drop side."

–Lamiel Oesterreicher

"I would not recommend cribs with hinged drops on the front. While they are certainly pretty, they are a huge safety hazard to little ones, whether they are trying to climb out and the latches give way (common), or they pinch their little hands and feet in the hinges. I also suggest checking the mattress support. Many manufacturers use cardboard supports, which weaken over time. Ever see a 2-year-old jumping up and down in a crib? Dangerous with the cardboard. My best advice is to check for a spring or solid wood support that will not give way over time."

–Megan Martin

✓ **Test the drop-down side before you buy. How easy is it to operate? You'll be lowering the side several times a day, so you want to make sure it works smoothly. Can it be done with one hand? Finally, what kind of sound does it make when you raise the side? The quieter the better, as there will be many times the baby will be asleep when you lay him down, and you'll want to be able to raise the crib side without waking him up.**

✓ **Consider whether or not you really need the extra features, like a drawer underneath the crib or the ability to convert it to a toddler bed. These extras make the crib more expensive, and you may not end up using them.**

"We chose the Babi Italia crib line. They were very stylish, very sturdy, and overall, I have been very pleased with my purchase. However, I would say that the convertible aspect of the crib was a bit less helpful than I imagined. We converted the cribs into toddler beds when my twins were able to crawl into the cribs with the side up. (My two never actually crawled out, but that was my fear.)

"What happened was that they found the bouncy crib, with the three tall sides and one open side to look more like a toddler trampoline and jungle gym than a bed. We were afraid of injuries from jumping to the

floor, so we tried putting down mats, and found they would often fall asleep anywhere in the room (including on the mats) but rarely on the beds.

"With space at a premium, two twin beds would take up too much room, and there was still the issue of the height from the floor, so we chose to buy toddler beds — Cosco brand. So far, these toddler beds have been wonderful. They are sturdy. They have a board under the crib mattress, so there is far less bounce, and it has reduced (though not eliminated) the bed jumping. They are low to the ground for the kids to get in and out of, and they look like real beds, so they are learning to sleep in beds and do things like make their beds in the morning. All in all, they have been a good purchase, and one we plan on using until the kids outgrow them and ask for a larger bed."

—THERESA SMEAD

✓ Check to see how easy it is to lower the mattress. You will have to do this several times as the baby begins to crawl, stand and, yes, even try to climb out of the crib. So you want a crib with a mattress support that's as easy to lower as possible.

✓ Snug and firm should be your watchwords when shopping for a mattress. You don't want any gaps between the mattress and the crib slats.

OUR FAVORITE BRAND

Pali

WHY WE LOVE IT

"After extensive research and price comparisons, I bought the Pali April crib. I considered buying an American-made crib, but after reading many reviews, I decided to get an Italian crib, as they are supposed to be the best-made cribs with the best release mechanisms. I found my Pali crib at my local affiliate of Baby News. They were having a $50 off sale. It made my crib just over $300. I found it to be a great value over the American-made cribs that were almost as much, but with fewer features. My Pali has three height settings and a great drawer built in beneath the crib for blankets, etc."

—BETH MILLER

"We bought a Pali crib. The price was really good, given the great quality. The thing I like most about Pali is that all of their hardware for the drop side is hidden."

–TARA TUCKER

"I am currently using a Pali crib for my daughter. When I went shopping for a crib, I looked for solid wood construction. I would advise a new or expecting mother when shopping for a crib to look for durability and function. I wanted easy, one-hand drop sides and a great mattress."

–LISA BITTAR

"I just love my three Pali cribs. They are Italian-made cribs, they have a drawer under the crib, the side can go down with just one hand and the use of the knee with a baby in your other hand. It's also a quiet crib. You can release the side and it won't wake up your baby. You can turn it into a toddler bed and even order a safety rail to use with the toddler bed."

–ANDREA SUISSA

"I've only had one crib (a Pali) and I love it. It is easy to get the side up and down. It is attractive. The sliding drawer is convenient and quiet and opens with a foot. It rolls, so it is easy to get dropped objects, and it really was easy to assemble."

–JENNIFER ROSE

Infant Car Seat

By now, you probably know that infant car seats come in two varieties: the bucket kind that comes with a separate base and the convertible car seat, which stays in the car and faces rear during the first year, then gets turned around to face forward once the baby is 20 pounds and one year old.

Your preference for which type of infant car seat is best may depend largely on how big your baby is. For example, if you have a small- to average-sized baby, you may enjoy the convenience of an infant car seat because it allows you to move the baby in and out of the car without waking him. Infant car seats also can be easily dropped into 'travel systems' or lightweight stroller frames, which effectively turn the car seat into a stroller, again without waking the baby. If you have a big baby, however, she may be too heavy to carry around in a bucket-style car seat. Moreover, your big baby will likely outgrow this type of seat before the first year is up, and you may end up having to buy a convertible car seat anyway.

✓ **Though most of us are fans of the travel systems, many infant car seats will fit into any full-sized stroller, so you don't necessarily have to buy a travel system in order to be able to move your sleeping baby from car seat to stroller without waking her.**

✓ **A downside to the travel systems is that they are bulky. A good alternative is a lightweight stroller frame, such as the Snap-N-Go by Baby Trend®.**

✓ **Always go for a seat with a five-point harness.**

✓ **Never buy a used car seat, such as from a yard sale. It may have been in an accident (you can't always tell), and car seats that have been in accidents should not be used again.**

✓ **If you buy a bucket-style infant seat, there's no need to buy another one if you have a second car. You can simply purchase an additional base.**

TOP PICK FOR INFANT CARRIER STYLE CAR SEAT

Graco SnugRide®

WHY WE LOVE IT

"I love the Graco SnugRide. It's easy to install, and it attaches to most Graco strollers. It also doubles as a carrier."

—LAMIEL OESTERREICHER

"We purchased a Graco SnugRide DX5. I really loved it. It had a fairly comfortable handle, a five-point harness, a stay-in-car base and received the highest rating from Consumer Reports. It also came in quite a few patterns/designs. At the time, I really liked having a car seat that could

go in and out of the car easily because my daughter would often fall asleep in the car and this way, I could take her inside or snap her into her stroller without necessarily waking her."

–STACEY SKLAR

"I recommend a Graco car seat because any Graco car seat will snap into any other Graco carriage. When I have another baby, I can buy a Graco double stroller and know my infant seat will fit. Also, I had a minor problem with a Graco product and their customer service department was fantastic. Graco is also the only company so far that I know makes a running stroller with an infant car seat. I got this and then purchased another Graco stroller for under $100 to use as my primary stroller. I also found that they carried a lot of different patterns."

–SUSAN DOBRATZ

"I really like the Graco SnugRide. It just seems to fit my baby better and is actually easier to get in and out of the car than the ones we had with our first two boys because of the lever located at the head of the seat. With the older ones, we had to move the handle back and forth to lock and unlock it."

–WENDY DOUGLAS

TOP PICK FOR CONVERTIBLE CAR SEAT

Britax Roundabout

WHY WE LOVE IT

"I absolutely love the Britax Roundabout. It is very safe and has gotten great reviews. I feel that for the safety of my son, I will spend a little more to get a good-quality seat. It has the five-point harness as well as a safety feature that helps stabilize the car seat in the car by attaching to the floor (or bottom of front seat) and to the car seat."

–ANNA MARIA JOHNSON

"The Britax Roundabout may be more expensive than some of the others, but it is well worth the price. Made in England, it exceeds all safety standards required in the U.S. It is made of a special material which makes it superior in its ability to sustain the impact of a crash. It can be used for a wider range of weights – rear-facing, it can be used up to 30 pounds., whereas most car seats have a limit of 20 pounds.

Front-facing, it can be used from 20 to 40 pounds. It also has a tether, and there are several cute fabric styles available."

–DIANE BEDROSIAN, M.D.

"I have a Britax Roundabout. I love it. It just seems to fit my daughter perfectly. It is also very easy to use. We have a different seat in daddy's car, and you can definitely tell the difference in quality. You can get both the Britax and the child secured tightly. It is worth the extra money. Britax also seems to stay ahead of the safety laws and therefore, your seat should last through more than one child."

–TIFFANY ZIMMER

"I'm so happy with our Britax Roundabout car seat. It is easy to install, easy to use and full of thoughtful touches, like the fabric disk that protects your baby's legs from the buckle when it gets hot from the sun, or the velcro that holds the straps out of the way while you put your baby in the seat. It's probably the priciest seat on the market, but it's well worth it!"

–RACHEL HULAN

"The Britax has received the highest consumer and product ratings overall and holds the infant from 15 to 40 pounds. We were able to keep our son rear-facing until he was 18 months old. Some seats do not allow such versatility."

–MONIQUE RIVERA-ROGERS

Stroller

When shopping for a stroller, consider how you'll use it. Will you use it mostly for walks to the park or trips to the mall? Jogging or for quick errands? There is a stroller made for each of these uses, and the features differ accordingly. Jogging strollers, for example, are hugely popular with joggers and walkers, but they don't have baskets, so they aren't useful for shopping or on trips where you need a place to store a big diaper bag. Full-size strollers are ideal for shopping, but can be bulky to take in and out of the car when you're running several errands. Umbrella strollers are lightweight, yet aren't suitable for babies who can't sit up yet. And lightweight stroller frames are perfect for any trips with infants, since you don't have to take them out of the car seat to put them in the stroller.

But they only last as long as the baby can ride in the infant carrier car seat. For our purposes, we'll focus here on the first stroller to buy and why we recommend it.

OUR TOP PICKS FOR YOUR FIRST STROLLER

1. Any brand of travel system (a standalone stroller, into which you can snap the infant car seat).
2. A lightweight stroller frame, such as Baby Trend®'s Snap-N-Go or Kolcraft®'s Universal Car Seat Carrier, into which you can snap a carrier-style infant car seat.

WHY WE LOVE THEM

"I makes so much sense if you use a stroller at all to have the combination. You can just click the baby in the car or in the stroller. The ease is amazing."

—AMELIA STINSON-WESLEY

"The Snap-N-Go is the most essential stroller for infants because it allows you to take a lovely sleeping child from the car in the car seat and attach the seat to the Snap-N-Go frame. For twins, another company just came out with a frame called the Double Decker™. It is great because it stacks one infant car seat on the top and the other on the bottom (narrow enough to fit down aisles). It is light to transport because it is just a frame (double strollers are so heavy)."

—BETH BLECHERMAN

"I like the Graco travel system because you don't have to wake your newborn when you put them in the stroller, and it will grow with the baby."

—BARBARA NICHOLS

"I have an Evenflo stroller, and I love it. I have the car seat/stroller combo and it has served me well over the past eight months. It is really easy to open and close and has shocks that make it a comfortable ride for her, no matter where we are. The only problem I have with it is that sometimes it is just too big to haul around. It fits okay in my trunk and I can fit other things in there too, but if I am going on a big shopping trip, I usually have to take it out."

—HEATHER MEININGER

"I recommend the Snap-N-Go for the first stroller. It's lightweight and easy to use because the infant car seat snaps right into it."

–JUDITH WU

"I recommend the lightest stroller you can find. Many moms develop back pain and extra fatigue from lugging things around. I like the ones that convert from stroller to car seat, so you don't have to wake the baby."

–BRENDA DINTIMAN, M.D.

"The combination strollers are the best in my opinion. Not only do you get the stroller, but you also get an infant car seat and carrier all in one. I would definitely recommend getting one of the lighter strollers, such as the Graco MetroLite. It can be a real hassle to fold a heavy stroller when you are already carrying a heavy child and a diaper bag."

–LAMIEL OESTERREICHER

"I used a Snap-N-Go at first. It was light and easy to load the frame in and out of the car, and a breeze to snap the car seat in and out."

–SHARON LICHTENFELD

Rocking Chair

For some of us, the best part about having a baby is spending hours in a rocking chair, feeding, reading and just comforting him. When shopping for a rocker, our most important advice is to try before you buy. Most of us love the glider rockers, but not everyone finds them comfortable. And what may be comfortable during pregnancy may not be comfortable once the baby is born. So if at all possible, test out the rocker/recliner early in your pregnancy before you have a huge belly. How does your back feel? What about your arms? Try it with a baby doll to see how your arms fit on the rocker while feeding the baby. Consider, too, how your spouse/partner fits in the rocker. If he'll be feeding the baby, he should be comfortable, too.

TIPS FROM THE TRENCHES

✓ **Save money on the stool. The footstool is extra and we're divided on whether or not it's worth it. Mostly,** we like the idea of having some sort of footstool, but we don't think you have to spend the money for a gliding ottoman. Consider buying a plain wooden footstool or nursing stool, especially if you don't plan to use the rocker in another room when the baby grows up.

✓ **Consider how you'll use it when comparing features.** Today's rocker recliners can come with everything from swivels to nursing stools to built-in vibrating massagers. Consider how and where you'll be using your rocker to see if these features are worth it. Most of us like the nursing stool feature, which allows your feet to rest on the ottoman at an angle. The swivel may be important if the rocker is next to a table and you want to turn to reach a glass of water or put down the bottle.

✓ **Look ahead two years when selecting fabric.** The fabrics for glider rockers have gotten much better in recent years, but most of them still look unmistakably "baby." Consider what you'll do with the glider when the baby outgrows it. Will you have another baby? Will you sell it? Will you move it to the living room or den? If you plan on moving it, buy a fabric to match the furniture in the other room. Another alternative is to recover the chair later.

OUR NUMBER ONE FAVORITE ROCKING CHAIR

Dutailier Glider Rocker

WHY WE LOVE IT

"I would definitely recommend the Dutailier glider with the glider ottoman. It's a beautifully-crafted glider and very sturdy. It's wide enough and sturdy enough for my husband who is a big guy, as well."

–KAREN HURST

"I recommend the glider with an ottoman. They are so comfortable and so nice to have for that middle-of-the-night feeding or screaming match.

The easy glide was so soothing to my son in the early months, and now I added it to my furniture in my living room."

—MICHELLE KOSEC

"Dutailier all the way! They are so comfy. I used to work in an infant retail store and I had a customer buy one for his daughter, and he came back the next week to buy one for himself because he thought it was more comfortable than his recliner. I'll keep mine forever."

—MARI KISTLER

"We bought the Dutailier glider rocker. We did not buy the accompanying ottoman. Instead, I purchased a simple nursing stool from BabyCenter.com for about $30. I love the chair and the stool."

—STACEY SKLAR

"I like the glider rockers. They have a nice cushioned seat and back that is comfortable to sit in for long periods of time."

—DEBBY MADRID

"The Dutailier is not only my favorite brand, but also one of my must-haves that I recommend to all my pregnant friends. Mine also reclines. I love it, love it, love it! I have used it to nurse, bond with and soothe my daughter over the last seven months and I hope to have it throughout her childhood."

—MICHELLE GEBHARD, D.O.

High Chair

You don't have to buy a high chair before the baby is born, but you will eventually need a high chair or some sort of feeding chair when the baby starts to eat solid food. We look for a chair that is well-constructed (read: safe), reclines (baby probably won't be able to sit up straight at the first feedings), completely washable (leave the wood chairs in the antique shops, please) and if space is a premium, can be stowed easily.

OUR TOP PICK (WARNING: IT'S PRICEY)

Peg-Pérego Prima Pappa

WHY WE LOVE IT

"We have the Peg-Pérego Prima Pappa. It's a super high chair, and because it's on wheels, the height of the seat is adjustable. It has a double tray for easy wash-ups, it folds up easily for storage, the seat reclines for bitty babies, it has a safety bar so that the baby can't slip out or turn around to stand up and it comes in lots of bright pretty patterns!"

–CARA VINCENS

"We have the 2002 model that also includes a removable dinner tray, but all of them have variable height positions and a reclining seat that is independent of the tray (all the others move the tray up when you recline). The colors are fashionable and fun (we have lime green and blue!), and the legs are made of metal that folds up (a real space-saver)."

–MICHELLE GEBHARD, D.O.

"I love the Peg-Pérego Prima Pappa high chair. It has great reclining positions, and I have been able to use it since birth! Madyson is able to be at the table with us, which I hope will help her with getting used to family meal time."

–LISA BITTAR

"I would recommend the Prima Pappa by Peg-Pérego. It's pretty pricey, but with all the features you get out of it, it's worth it. It has many reclining positions and height positions, which make it nice to change as needed for whichever eating situation you're in. It folds up to be about six inches wide, which makes it nice if you need to put it away after each use, and you don't have a ton of space. It's fairly easy to clean, and the chair pad is removable for easier cleaning, as well."

–KAREN HURST

A GREAT INEXPENSIVE ALTERNATIVE

A portable booster seat such as the Portable 3-in-1 Booster Seat by The First Years® or the Safety 1st Fold N Go Booster

WHY WE LOVE THESE

"The Safety 1st booster seat with attached tray is my only 'high chair.' I never purchased a high chair because we have a small kitchen, and I didn't want to take up the extra floor space with a chair that my children would outgrow in a matter of months. My kids began sitting in the

booster at around 6 months (we do introduce solid food – cereal – before 6-months-old and use the bouncy seat as a feeding station before moving them to the booster). Between 12 and 18 months, we remove the tray and begin using the booster seat alone and pull it up to the table. The booster chair comes apart easily for washing and can be folded for travel. I cannot recommend it highly enough as a high chair substitute or as a toddler/preschooler booster at your table."

–SIDNEY MARKS

"I use the Portable 3-in-1 Booster Seat. It's inexpensive, and you can take it anywhere. Plus, some of the parts can be cleaned in the dishwasher."

–LEAH CHEW

"I actually returned my beautiful, but very impractical, wooden high chair because we liked this one (The First Years 3-in-1 Booster) so much. The seat reclines to three different positions, eventually, we can sit her at the table with no tray because it is attached to a chair, we have yet to find a chair it won't fit on…even our chair outside at the patio table, both the seat and tray are dishwasher safe, the seat pad is super easy to take off and can be used without the pad, it's lightweight, and my 3-year-old niece loves to sit in it when she is here. I like that it is able to grow so well with a child."

–SUSAN DOBRATZ

"I have a Safety 1st booster seat with tray. Works great and doesn't take up any extra room. Perfect for a small space. When baby gets older, just remove the tray and push him up to the table."

–NICOLE LUCIER

Bottles

Even if you're nursing, you may need bottles for when you go back to work or when you go out. The key to buying bottles is to try them on the baby first. Some babies seem to do better with one type of bottle, if say, they have reflux or they tend to be gassy. Other babies have a preference for one type of nipple, and you may have to try a few before discovering the one that works for your baby.

Avent®

WHY WE LOVE THEM

"I used the Avent bottles, and I liked them the best. I have exclusively breastfed my baby since birth, and the Avent bottles were the only ones that we didn't have a problem with as far as nipple confusion."

–HEATHER MEININGER

"I love the Avent system because of the flexibility. Each bottle size attaches to the same handles, nipples, sippy cup attachments and lids. Each part can be used with any other part. The babies loved these bottles and learned to hold their bottles by 6-months-old because the handles made it so easy."

–SUSAN LONERGAN

"The Avent bottles are very durable and easy to clean."

–CHAYA JAMIE REICH

"The Avent bottles are the best! They are the only brand whose nipples didn't collapse when my daughter drank from them. They also have a wide opening at the top, which makes it super easy to put formula in."

–STEPHANIE HOSSZU

"The Avent bottle is supposed to help or prevent colic and has a slow flow nipple that is great for breastfed babies. Finally, the shape of the nipple is more like a breast."

–CLAIRE BIENVENU

"If breastfeeding, I liked the Avent system. They make a good breast pump and you can just pump directly into the bottles for use later in the day. The bottles can be converted into sippy cups by adding a sippy nipple and handles to the bottle itself."

–TRACI BRAGG, M.D.

Formula

You and your baby's doctor can decide which specific formula to use, but we can help you decide whether to choose powder, concentrate or ready-to-feed.

OUR FAVORITE TYPE

Powder

WHY WE PREFER IT

"I like to use powder because it is cheaper, more compact and doesn't spoil."

–RIVKA STEIN, M.D.

"I love the powder. I fill the bottles and put them out on the counter. When the baby is ready, all I have to do is grab one and add the powder, stir it up and we're ready to go. I never have to bother with heating up bottles (room temperature is fine), and at 2 a.m., this is a really good thing! It's also very handy when you're out and about to not have to worry about finding somewhere to heat up your formula."

–STACI PARO

"We prefer powder formula. We're on the run a lot, and it's safer and easier to mix fresh bottles as we need them."

–DEBBIE PALMER

"I use powder. It is less costly, doesn't go bad (until a month after the can is opened), and since you can make so much formula with one large can, there are less trips to the store."

–STEPHANIE R. SMITH

"I prefer powder formula for a few reasons. It's the most economical. If you spill powder formula, just wipe it up. The canned stuff stains if you don't rinse it out quickly. Also, the powder is easier to store: It takes up less space, and once it's opened, you don't have to put it in the refrigerator. Just cover it back up and put it back in the cupboard. And it's a lot easier than dealing with a can opener and trying to keep cold leftover formula or throwing it out and just wasting it while you're on the go."

–K. SCARLETT SHAW

First Cup

We recommend starting your baby on a cup as early as possible – 5 or 6 months is a good time. She may not be able to do much with it at first, but it will help her to get used to the cup, so it will be easier to transition from the bottle or breast.

OUR TOP PICK

Playtex® Spill-Proof Cup (sippy cup)

WHY WE LOVE IT:

"I like this brand because it is the absolute best spill-proof sippy cup. I've tried other brands that claim to be spill-proof, and they have leaked, or it was very difficult for my child to suck out the drink. The Playtex brand is also very easy to clean — just remove the valve and put both the cup and the valve in the dishwasher. I also like that Playtex offers a variety of cup sizes ranging from six ounces to the 12-ounce 'Big Sipster'."

—STEPHANIE MARTIN

"Playtex is a good brand. The valves are easy to clean and they make them in attractive colors and styles."

—MARI KISTLER

"I used the Playtex cup with the handles on the side. It was easy for my daughter to grip and hold on to, and it worked great."

—DEBBY MADRID

Baby Clothes

With baby clothes, it's a matter of balancing fashion with cost and durability. To save money, we shop the sales, scour outlets, go to consignment stores and shop at the end of the season for the next year.

OUR TOP TEN FAVORITE BRANDS OF BABY CLOTHES

1. Carter's
2. Baby Gap
3. Old Navy
4. OshKosh B'Gosh
5. Gymboree
6. Target
7. Wal-Mart®
8. The Children's Place
9. Little Me
10. Lands' End

WHY WE LOVE THEM

"I really like Carter's. They are a bit expensive, but they are really well made. They are also quite cute, and a good number of outfits are gender neutral, so they can be handed down between brothers and sisters."

—CHELSEA COFFEY HAMMAN

"I adore Carter's clothing for infants. They wash incredibly well, and they come in some of the most adorable prints and patterns. For my toddler, I get OshKosh B' Gosh when I can. They seem to wear well and wash great. Plus, he looks adorable in overalls."

—HEATHER HENDRICKSON

"I love the sale racks at Baby Gap for the hip and trendy, functional stuff."

—STACEY SKLAR

"We love Carter's clothing. You can find it almost anywhere, but we shop at a Carter's outlet near our home. I have found little in the way of good-looking boys clothing that does not have teddy bears, cars or footballs. Carter's does carry those types of clothing, but carries a line with bugs and turtles and dragonflies as well. It washes well, doesn't fade and runs a little big, so that Noah can wear it longer."

—DANA A. CROY

"I like Carter's baby clothes because they're affordable, practical (designed with snaps in all the right places for easy diaper changes and pulling over those little fragile heads) and because it's easy to build a baby's 'wardrobe' with all the basics you need (towels, undershirts, onesies, etc.). Plus, the cotton is soft next to baby's skin."

—JENNIFER YOUNG

"After trying many brands, Gap is still our favorite brand of clothes for Jack. When I was putting together a bag of clothes that Jack had outgrown for a girlfriend of mine, his Gap clothes were the only ones worth passing down! They withstand washing in hot (and often), which is really important."

—TIFFANY K. PRICE

"I love Gap and Gymboree...clothes that last forever and return policies are flexible. Oh yeah, and the sale prices are incredible. These stores can be found in most shopping malls, which is great if Grandma wants to buy something for her."

—CHANTAL LAURIN

"I ADORE Old Navy. The clothes are like adult clothes in smaller sizes. And the baby stuff is so cute. And the bargain racks are amazing. I buy coats for under $10 and put them away for next year."

–KATE STEIMAN

"I love Baby Gap. The quality can't be beat, and I know that it will stick around for future kids. If all else fails, it sells well on eBay!"

–ERIKA PLODZIEN

"I love hitting the clearance racks at Baby Gap and Gymboree. The selection is still good and I can easily shop ahead for the next year or season while I save up to 70 percent."

–SUSAN DOBRATZ

"I get my little girl's clothes from Wal-Mart (brand is Faded Glory). They are cute just like any other brand, but they are cheaper, which is important since they grow out of them so fast."

–AMANDA MARBREY

"Wal-Mart has the best prices and a large selection. Target has a good selection, but the clothes cost more than Wal-Mart. Gap is expensive, but their clothes are the best. Very soft and with extra cuteness."

–LEAH CHEW

"I really like The Children's Place because the prices are reasonable, the quality is great and they are adorable."

–ANITA GOOD

"I like OshKosh, only because all of my hand-me-downs have lasted so long – through three kids."

–ELICIA MOORE

"I really like the clothes I have found at Wal-Mart. They are durable and reasonably-priced."

–WENDY DOUGLAS

"I love Lands' End. The clothes are so well-made. They are sized so that my children always got more than one year of wear out of them. Because they are so well-constructed, I am able to pass down clothing that has been worn two-to-three seasons to the next child, who will also wear them two-to-three seasons."

–JULIE BARTLETT

THE BEST SOURCE FOR DESIGNER BABY CLOTHES AT GREAT PRICES — (WE CALL IT "THE BEST KEPT SECRET IN BABY FASHION")

eBay

WHY WE LOVE IT

"I buy most of my son's clothes on eBay. I can get almost new name-brand clothes for almost nothing. My best buy was a group of eight brand new outfits (still with the tags) from The Children's Place for $30."

—SARA HAMMONTREE

Baby Gear

There's no shortage of products on the market to make life easier for you and your little one. The trick is figuring out which ones are worth the money. Below are our top ten favorites, but keep in mind that baby gear is pretty subjective — what one mom considers a luxury, another might consider a necessity, depending on cost, lifestyle and your baby's habits and preferences.

OUR TOP TEN LIST OF "MUST HAVE" BABY PRODUCTS

1. Baby-Björn® front carrier
2. Sling
3. Battery-operated swing
4. Bouncy seat
5. Exersaucer
6. Boppy® pillow
7. Lightweight stroller frame, such as the Baby Trend Snap-N-Go
8. Backpack
9. Pack 'N Play®
10. Diaper Genie®★

★Editor's Note: The Diaper Genie also appears on our list of Four Products To Avoid (p.56). It seems that just as many moms love it as hate it. If you want to try something like the Diaper Genie that promises to be easier to use and more versatile, check out the

new Diaper Dekor. Most of us had our babies before this product came out, so we can't review it first-hand, but we have heard that it is easy to use (step on the pedal and toss in the diaper), can hold up to 480 newborn diapers and can be used as a regular trash can when your kids are finished with diapers.

WHY WE LOVE THEM

"The Baby-Björn® is sturdy and secure. I always feel safe when my baby is in it. And it helps my back a lot by not putting so much pressure on it."

—AMELIA STINSON-WESLEY

"It's wonderful to be able to carry your baby everywhere and still have your arms free. As young infants, my sons liked to snuggle next to my chest in the Baby-Björn facing me, and when they grew older, they loved to face outward to see the world around us. The Baby Bjorn fit both my body and my husband's body easily and comfortably. We took it everywhere."

—SUSAN TACHNA

"Even now that my baby is 9 months old, I find myself grabbing the baby carrier (Baby-Björn) much more readily than I do the stroller as I'm running out the door to do errands. A stroller can be cumbersome and sometimes difficult to navigate (depending on where you're going), whereas a baby on your person is easy, convenient and bond-cultivating. Half the time, the baby wants out of the stroller anyway, and I need to carry her with my two hands. If I have the carrier with me, I get the baby against my chest and my hands to myself."

—CAREN SADIKMAN, M.D.

"I love the Baby-Björn. I wish I invented it. You really don't feel the weight of the baby on your back; somehow it really evenly distributes it."

—ANDREA SUISSA

"We absolutely adore our baby sling. Having an infant that wanted to be carried ALL the time, I thought I would go crazy. But with the sling, I am able to carry Hana as much as she needs me to, while keeping my hands free at the same time. You can hold the baby in a variety of different positions, depending on if it's nap time, looking-around time or nursing time."

—SALLY FARRINGTON

"I recommend a good sling (Maya Wrap is the most popular). Babies can be carried hands free, can breastfeed discreetly on demand and it doesn't take up space!"

—MEGAN MILES

"I love the Maya Wrap sling. You can use it from newborn to 25 to 40 pounds. You can cradle hold, front carry (like a kangaroo), hip carry or back carry. When the seat belt on a shopping cart is broken, use the Wrap instead. It also makes a great light blanket. You don't have to take the baby out of it to put it in the car seat. That makes it great for when the baby has fallen asleep."

—BRENDA BROWN

"I absolutely loved my baby sling by NoJo. I used it from the time they were newborns up through the toddler years. It allows you to carry your baby in several different positions and is great for nursing. The wonderful thing is it allows you to keep your hands free for other things. This is especially helpful if your little one has colic. You can hold them close to you while still getting things done. It's also nice to have your hands free for chasing your other kids!"

—ANGELA SNODGRASS

"A swing is a must! We prefer the open-top, battery-operated kind. The swing saved our sanity many times when our son had colic."

—DEBBIE PALMER

"The swing helped calm my fussy, colicky baby and was almost the only way I could get her to take a nap, so I could attend to other things. The nice thing about it was that it kept going unless I turned it off, and I didn't have to rewind it every ten minutes, so the baby just kept on sleeping."

—JULIE BARTLETT

"My son wouldn't sleep in his crib from the time he was 1 month old to about 2-1/2 months. Don't ask me why; he just didn't. Without that swing, my husband and I would have gone insane. I think it not only soothed him, but the constant sound also soothed me to sleep."

—ANITA GOOD

"You need a baby swing. There are countless times that I have tried to calm my babies, and the swing was my savior. You need to have a battery-operated one; you don't want to have to get up every time the wind-up one dies down. I bought a Century two-speed swing for $50 at Wal-Mart."

—LEAH CHEW

"I used the bouncy seat to feed my daughter when she was too small to really sit in a high chair. And when we brought her home from the

hospital, it was perfect for her to sit upright in on those nights she didn't want to go to sleep in her crib."

–APRIL MCCONNELL

"A vibrating bouncy seat would be my top pick. Make sure to get the toy bar on it. Your baby will live in it for about three to four months. They can see things, they can be soothed with the vibrator when they're unhappy, they can be easily moved when necessary. I couldn't have survived without mine."

–STACEY STEVENS

"I think the item I probably used more than anything else when my daughter was born was the bouncy seat that vibrates. She had many happy hours in it. She even slept in it at night for the first three months."

–BARBARA NICHOLS

"My kids loved the bouncy seat, and you can move it from room to room very easily, unlike a swing. I used to put the bouncy seat in the bathroom when I took a shower, so I could still see them."

–SHERRY RENNIE

"The Exersaucer has to be number one from 4 months to 8-1/2 months old. My son just loved it. It gave him some independence. He could bounce up and down, turn around or just sit and play with his toys."

–NICOLE LUCIER

"I loved the activity center [Exersaucer] by Graco. He had all sorts of toys to play with, and it strengthened his legs at the same time. And Mommy could actually get things done while he was in it!"

–KATHLEEN CONROY

"I like the UltraSaucer [Exersaucer]. My son is 4 months old and has been using it since he was 3 months old, and he loves it! He is able to jump up and down, which strengthens his legs, and he loves all of the toys. He grabs and plays with them, and I really feel it is helping him tremendously with visual stimulation and his motor skills."

–JENNIFER CLEVELAND

"The Boppy pillow comes in handy for breastfeeding. It also works as a great prop for baby to take naps and it aids in helping the baby sit up."

–VERONICA WILSON

"My Boppy is so wonderful. My son just laid on it comfortably, and it gave my arms and breasts support. I still use it now even though I'm not nursing to give a bottle or even for me to lay my head on when lying down."

–ANNA MARIA JOHNSON

"The Boppy pillow saved my back and was nice to have the baby's body on something soft."

–HOLLY COCCHIOLA

"I recommend the Snap-N-Go. You just take the infant carrier and snap it to the stroller frame. It was so much easier and lighter than the heavy, bulky travel stroller. You can easily travel with it, and it won't take up too much room in the trunk."

–JUDITH WU

"Although the Snap-N-Go only lasts as long as the infant car seat (6 to 12 months, depending on baby's size), it is worth its weight in gold during that time period. It is so much easier to just take the Snap-N-Go out of the car and plop the sleeping baby in his/her car seat right into the Snap-N-Go, rather than either unfold a bulky combo stroller and/or risk waking the baby during the transfer. The combo strollers don't tend to be very good all-around strollers once the baby is bigger, so it's actually cheaper to buy the Snap-N-Go, then invest in a high-quality everyday stroller for when the baby is bigger. Make sure to get the deluxe version with the attached basket. New moms have no idea how much stuff they'll be lugging around. Getting a unit without the basket will cause you to hate the thing."

–STACEY STEVENS

"If you are at all outdoorsy and like to hike, walk the beach or go on terrain that isn't suitable for a stroller, I'd get a backpack. We take ours to the zoo, amusement parks, fairs and carnivals because it is sometimes a pain to maneuver a stroller in and out of doorways and through crowds. The backpack eliminates this problem and baby is up high and has a good view, too."

–STEPHANIE MARTIN

"A backpack carrier is not only for walks, but for doing housework as well. There were many evenings that the only way to make dinner was to put the baby in the backpack carrier while I cooked. The hours just before and during dinner usually are the fussiest for babies. Being carried on mommy's back helps to keep them calm."

–JULIE BARTLETT

"A Pack 'N Play with the bassinet and changing station has been truly a lifesaver for the other side of the house and for traveling."

–LAMIEL OESTERREICHER

"I like the Pack 'N Play. It's been helpful to have an enclosed area in which the baby can sleep and play, other than the crib, especially if you have a two-level home. The crib is upstairs and the play yard is downstairs. When babies are little and relatively immobile, you can put them down to sleep on any floor. But as they get older, and they may begin crawling quietly the minute they wake up from a nap, it's good to know that they're in a safe space."

–CAREN SADIKMAN, M.D.

"We live in a condo, and the Diaper Genie is a MUST for any apartment dweller. It holds a few days worth of diapers, and there is no odor."

–TIFFANY K. PRICE

"They weren't kidding when they said you would use up to 100 diapers a week. The Diaper Genie keeps you from running out to empty the garbage five times a day."

–GENEVIEVE MOLLOY

"A Diaper Genie is a must. We used ours up until the diapers got too big (sizes three and four). The lack of odor in the baby's room makes the Diaper Genie superior to diaper pails."

–DANIELLE MARION-DOYLE

THE THREE NURSING ACCESSORIES WE CAN'T LIVE WITHOUT

1. Boppy pillow
2. A good electric breast pump – we recommend the Medela Pump In Style®
3. Nursing pads

"One of the greatest things we purchased was a Boppy pillow. It puts the baby at just the right height to nurse, and it is machine-washable (a big plus). Initially, I couldn't live without nursing pads either, as leaking was a problem until my supply was well-established. After the first couple of months, though, I no longer needed the nursing pads. The Boppy is

still in use for nursing and for a support pillow as Hana is learning to sit up. It's a wonderful thing to have."

—MICHELLE LANEY

"The Boppy pillow is great. I mean, come on, you're exhausted, unsure of what you're doing, etc. The last thing you should be worried about is supporting the baby's entire weight every time you feed it. You need to learn how to get latched on first, the support will come later."

—STEPHANIE R. SMITH

"The Medela breast pump is an absolute must! For many products in this world, there are several quality brands to choose from and little difference between them. With breast pumps, however, it has been my observation that everyone loves Medela and struggles with all the other ones. I bought a car cigarette-lighter adapter for mine, and I was able to pump on the road. My pump enabled me to breastfeed for two years with little inconvenience."

—SARAH PLETCHER

"The Medela Pump In Style is a must for working moms who pump. It is fast, discreet and efficient."

—CLAIRE BIENVENU

"I bought the top-of-the-line Medela Pump In Style. I love it. It has helped me through sore nipples, engorgement, etc. It also guarantees that I can get out of the house. There is no reason to buy a new Pump In Style, however. Medela strongly discourages buying and selling used pumps and says it is unsanitary to use a pump someone else has used. Baloney! It is very easy to buy new breast cups, tubes and bottles, and the milk never gets near the motor – EVER! You should feel comfortable buying a used one from a friend or off of eBay."

—TARA TUCKER

"My favorite nursing accessory is my breast pump. I use the Medela Pump In Style, which is stylish, lightweight and easy to take anywhere. I use it not only to express milk while at work, but also to increase my milk supply quickly when the baby grows (I just pump in between feedings for a couple of days."

—RIVKA STEIN, M.D.

"Nursing pads are a must. I leaked everywhere if my baby slept more than three hours."

—LEAH CHEW

"The pump gave me freedom to go out with my husband or a friend, and it helped my babies to be able to have someone else feed them once in awhile."

–ANN STOWE

"Lansinoh disposable breast pads absorbed wonderfully, and I sure felt confident wearing them. I also loved my Medela Pump In Style breast pump and Avent hand pump. I couldn't have breastfed as long as I did without them."

–HEATHER FRENCH

AND FOUR PRODUCTS TO AVOID

1. Inefficient, manual breast pumps
2. Crib comforters
3. Wipe warmer
4. Diaper Genie★

Editor's Note: The Diaper Genie also appears on our Top Ten List of "Must Have" Baby Products, see page 49 to find a good alternative.

"Avoid cheap manual breast pumps like the plague! They are painful, don't work and can even damage your breast tissue! If you must pump, use an Avent Isis™ for occasional pumping or a Medela Pump In Style if you are returning to work."

–MEGAN MILES

"You should never buy an inexpensive breast pump. You don't want to have to manually control the timing of the suction, and you certainly don't want to pump manually. Buy the best pump you can afford and one that suits your needs. If you are going to be pumping every day for a long period of time (like if you go back to work), then you will probably want a higher-quality pump that will stand up to long-term use."

–STEPHANIE ZARA

"Avoid buying the cute crib comforters that match the crib bedding. These things are totally useless since it's not safe to use on the baby, due to suffocation potential, so it's just a waste of money."

–REBECCA HARPER

"My girlfriend used a wipe warmer and found that whenever they were out and about and having to use unwarmed wipes, her son screamed."

—TIFFANY K. PRICE

"I did not like the Diaper Genie. I thought it was too difficult to change the bags, and sometimes I couldn't get the diapers to 'sausage' by twisting, so diapers were just all running into each other. I prefer the Diaper Champ since it uses regular trash bags."

—BETH MILLER

"The Diaper Genie is not worth the money. Probably 90% of the people I have talked to that have one never used it or only used it for a short amount of time. I found that plastic bags or even the special scented ones that cost like $2.99 for 100 are a lot better. Dirty diapers go out that day and don't stink up your house."

—BROOKE ULINSKI

"The Diaper Genies are pretty expensive (and so are the refills), and they seemed to still leave a smell. I would recommend just buying the baby-scented bags for the stinky diapers. They are cheaper and work better."

—DEBBIE PALMER

THE BABY PRODUCT WE WISH SOMEONE WOULD INVENT

"A machine that interprets baby's cries, so you know EXACTLY what's wrong!"

—KEL BRIGHT

"An automatic diaper changer."

—AMANDA MARBREY

"An automatic machine that rocks your baby back to sleep when they get fussy. It will go off as soon as the baby makes the slightest sound, and gently rock him back to sleep or make him more comfortable."

—MARI KISTLER

"A robot to fetch me diapers, bottles, wipes and such!"

—BECKY GASTON

"An easier-to-carry baby seat. Those are a killer to use."

—BRENDA DINTIMAN, M.D.

"A better way to bathe a newborn. Babies are so slippery, so I switched to sponge baths unless someone was here to help me. A sling or something that fits into the baby bath would be ideal. Something that cradles them and supports their head."

–TIFFANY K. PRICE

"A larger bouncy seat. I have big babies, so the ones that exist now don't last very long."

–WENDY DOUGLAS

"An infant tub that somehow keeps the shallow water at the same temperature as you put it in. They cool so quickly and I had a baby who loved the bath. We had to drain a little, add a little, drain a little, add a little...it was a pain."

–SUSAN DOBRATZ

"Something that cleans and makes the bottles."

–BROOKE ULINSKI

"A crystal ball that showed you that all the hard work, all the sleepless nights and all the smelly diapers are not in vain when you see all the love you have given for so long is returned to you tenfold."

–KELI LOVELAND

"A stroller with a mini fridge. Hey, I can dream, can't I? It's a nice idea for those long days at the park."

–BOBBI ANNAL

CHAPTER 4:

Shopping for Baby: Where to Buy

As moms of little ones, our criteria for what makes a good shopping experience may differ from what we looked for before we had babies. For example, we want stores that are easily accessible. If you can't get there, shop, and be back in time for the baby's afternoon nap, it's too far.

Selection is important – not just because we like having choices, but because we don't have the time or energy to schlep around town to different stores to get what we need.

And prices better be competitive. This stuff doesn't come cheap! It doesn't hurt if we can get other shopping done at the same time. Any store that offers a good selection of baby products plus other household necessities is invariably more attractive to us, since we can't buzz in and out of stores as easily as we used to anymore.

OUR THREE FAVORITE STORES FOR BABY PRODUCTS

1. Babies "R" Us®
2. Wal-Mart®
3. Target

WHY WE LOVE THEM

"I definitely recommend Babies "R" Us. They are expensive, but they always have what I'm looking for."

–ERIKA PLODZIEN

"We just go to Wal-Mart. You can find pretty much anything there that you can find elsewhere, and it's usually at a better price."

–K. SCARLETT SHAW

"Babies "R" Us a huge selection of stuff. Plus I like the fact that they have special pregnant women parking spaces!"

–KATE STEIMAN

"My favorite store to shop for baby items so far has been Target. They carry a variety of different items, have lots of things for the nursing mom, and their prices seem to be extremely competitive. They carry toys, clothes, diapers, etc. – basically everything you need."

–SALLY FARRINGTON

"I go to Wal-Mart. I am a stay-at-home-mom and my husband is in the Army, so money is usually really tight. I can get their brand of diapers; wipes are cheaper there; and I can get my baby's food, formula, clothes, basically anything I need for him all in one trip."

–KELLY HARDEN

"My favorite store right now is Target. I shop at Target for baby products, toys, kids' clothes, etc. The reason I love Target so much is that I can get everything I need in one stop. Target generally has a good selection of items in stock at the right price. I appreciate the fact that I don't have to drive all over town to find things, and the 90-day return policy is great."

–SIDNEY MARKS

SHOPPING ONLINE

The Internet offers all the same benefits as catalog shopping – access to all the newest, most creative and unusual baby products, the ability to shop from home at any time of the day or night – plus a few more: great prices (in some cases), access to a wealth of product information and reviews (check out Epinions.com) and the ability to hop from store to store within minutes to find the best deals.

THE TWO BEST WEB SITES FOR BABY PRODUCTS

1. BabyCenter.com®
2. eBay.com®

WHY WE LOVE THEM

"I love BabyCenter. Not only do they have a store with tons of items for sale, but they also have bulletin boards where moms can post questions to other moms with babies that are born in the same month and year. It has been wonderful when discussing such issues as breastfeeding, table foods, teeth, ear infections and many milestones."

–STEPHANIE R. SMITH

"BabyCenter's selection and pricing are good, and the service is quick and reliable. The information available on the site is extremely helpful and the chat rooms are nice, too. My older son was born in 1996, before the dot.com explosion and before BabyCenter existed. I had many different pregnancy/baby books taking up space on my shelves and ran around to many different stores shopping for baby gear. When my second son was born in the summer of 1999, I found that I no longer needed any of the baby books I owned and no longer needed to run around to various stores in my free time. I could get all the information I wanted and all the gear, too, from BabyCenter. Furthermore, I could shop online at times like 2 a.m., after a nighttime feeding, when all was quiet and I had no other family demands."

–SUSAN TACHNA

"I'm an eBay addict. I have found some great deals on gently-used baby items. I got my son's entire crib bedding for under $30 there, and it looked brand new. You can find just about anything there...toys, clothes, bedding, nursery items and many more."

–VERONICA WILSON

"I know it sounds silly, but eBay has EVERYTHING for a good price."

–TRACY PRITCHARD

CHAPTER 5:

Preserving Memories

While we're going through it, the sleepless nights, poopy diapers and teething pain may seem like it will never end. But the baby years go by in a flash, and if you don't record the memorable moments, you may forget them.

Our Favorite Ways to Preserve Memories from the Baby Years

1. Baby book
2. Scrapbook
3. Pictures
4. Baby's handprint or footprint
5. Keepsake box
6. Journal
7. Video
8. Calendar
9. Time capsule
10. Bronzing shoes or other mementos

WHAT WE LOVE ABOUT THEM

"I just have a normal baby book and a Peter Rabbit keepsake box. It's huge and it has little compartments in it for the little stuff like teeth or keeping the umbilical cord. Also, they have these little things that are called Baby Memories that you can get from Wal-Mart. It's where you make a mold of your baby's food or hand. I did both."

—AMANDA MARBREY

"I have a baby memory book for each child and have tried to keep up with it as new teeth come in, new words are spoken and more milestones are reached. Another good idea are boxes, which I found at Wal-Mart, in which to keep baby's memory items. They are cute — the ones I have for my girls have a Winnie the Pooh design. They have a place on the front

for a photo of your baby. Open up the box, and there is a large storage space for baby items, such as first shoes or favorite clothing or whatever you choose. There is a small area with little drawers and a sturdy envelope attached to the inside cover, in which to store smaller items. "One thing to do when they are newborns is clay or tile handprints and/or footprints. There are many shops around where you can do them yourself, i.e., you do the prints on clay, then the store will fire/glaze them for you. There are also some specialty stores that will do the entire process for you at a fairly reasonable price. I have seen these offered at kiosks in the local mall, and a woman also comes to our local Babies "R" Us on the weekends to do this."

–DIANE BEDROSIAN, M.D.

"I have a standard Winnie the Pooh baby book with fill-in-the-blanks. But I also have two photo albums full of pictures, cards and trinkets from my daughter's first year. I have a digital camera with almost 1,000 pictures that have been taken mostly since she was born. For every picture in each album, I have done a handwritten caption, with wording that indicates she is talking. One says, 'I love hanging out with Daddy. He's soooo cool!' I took a new picture every month since her first birthday and I made a collage of all twelve months using just her face from each picture. You can really see how she changed from birth to one year."

–COLLEEN GRACE WEAVER

"Hallmark puts out an adorable book. It is a three-ring binder and has pages for all kinds of written and tangible mementos. It helps you record things you never even thought to think about! It comes with photo album pages, blank pages and even special sections for adopting parents. And because it's a three-ring binder, you can add anything of your own that you like. My nanny just gave my husband and me an anniversary card with my baby's footprints and handprints on it. She painted the baby's hands and feet with fingerpaint and then stamped them on the card. I cried when I saw it. An inexpensive, yet priceless gift."

–CAREN SADIKMAN, M.D.

"I use Creative Memories and other scrapbooking brands to preserve pictures/photos and special days/moments. I draw outlines of my child's hands each month and do handprints (using a colored ink pad) every now and then. I love the casts of baby's foot and/or hands, but have had no luck at all using a variety of products. They are not for squirmy babies."

–AMELIA STINSON-WESLEY

"I really enjoy scrapbooking. It allows me to mix photos and memorabilia, such as hospital wristbands or locks of hair from the first haircut. It's also a fun way to spend my time and lots of moms do it, so it's a good conversation starter."

–STEPHANIE HOSSZU

"Scrapbooking is my favorite way to preserve memories. I have a scrapbook for each of my children and have gone away on a scrapbooking weekend with my friends. My children love looking at their scrapbooks and get excited to see each new page that I make. I make pages for Christmas, Halloween, birthdays, vacations and other special events. I have used Creative Memories products and have had one of their shows at my home. Scrapbooking products can be purchased at Michaels, Hallmark stores, Wal-Mart and specialty scrapbooking stores."

–KIMBERLY MERCURIO, M.D.

"I am a scrapbook fanatic. I have been doing it almost four years, and I love it. It is a very creative way to keep pictures and preserve them in such a beautiful way. At first, I thought cutting into my pictures was a horrible thing, but when my aunt showed me her albums, I was so impressed with just how adorable the pictures turned out, all decorated with stickers and die cuts. My favorite place to go shopping for scrapbook supplies is Wal-Mart or Michaels."

–VERONICA WILSON

"I am currently making a Creative Memories album. I love it because it is a photo album and scrapbook in one. I have everything in there from his hospital bracelet to photos to his birth announcement, etc. I am doing it for his first year. Then a separate album for ages 2 to 5, then school, etc. This way, you have everything together instead of a scrapbook and a million photo albums. I am also doing a wall portrait hanging; I used the template for school (the one with twelve small spaces for pictures and a large space in the middle). I put every month's 'birthday' picture in each of the twelve openings, and then on his first birthday, that photo will go in the middle."

–JENNIFER CLEVELAND

"I keep a calendar handy and jot notes into it daily. Then I can sit down and transfer all their cute things when I have time to get out the albums. Otherwise, I forget what happened by the time I am able to get out the major memento-savers!"

–DENISE GREENWOOD, M.D.

"I keep a calendar above the changing table where I list everything the baby does and every milestone. It's easy, cheap, cute if you choose a nice calendar and a great way to preserve memories throughout the year."

–LAURENCE THELLIER

"My parents live across the country, and we bought them a Ceiva [brand] Internet picture frame to preserve and share precious memories of their grandkids. Since my folks don't own or use computers and don't want to learn, I had no way of emailing them photos. With this simple product, they set up an electronic picture frame in their home, and each night, the frame uses their phone line to check for photos I have sent them over the Internet. If there are photos, the frame uploads them automatically. In the morning, my parents can see what the kids are up to in photos flashing on the frame in a screenshow. Using my digital camera, I can get pictures to my folks in minutes if I want to. For example, I can take a digital photo of my kids holding up a 'Happy Birthday Grandma' sign and send it to Grandma so it is waiting for her when she wakes up on her birthday. Fun!

"The product requires purchase of the frame and then an annual subscription, but it is not that expensive, and I know it is the best gift I have ever given my parents. They love it, and so do their friends. People are always asking my mother if there is anything new on her frame. They actually come visit to see new photos!"

–SUSAN LONERGAN

"I love memory boxes or chests because you can store special outfits and such in them. I also think memory books/scrapbooks are special. I made a baby handprint out of homemade play clay with my daughter when she turned one. It was really special because we made it together instead of buying one."

–BECKY GASTON

"I have a big box that looks like a book, but snaps closed, which matches my son's nursery theme (John Lennon Real Love). Inside, it has some drawers and a pouch, and I just throw things in there. He also had a matching calendar for Baby's First Year that came with stickers to mark milestones, and you could fill out each page with details of baby's development. There was also space for a picture at birth and one year."

–MICHELE LONGENBACH

"I keep a journal that I write letters to each of my girls in about once a month. I love to read back in it to see how I was feeling or the funny things they said."

–SABRINA LANE

"The main thing I do is write. I often write a funny or telling story about my children, email it to friends and family and save a copy in my files. I augment that with a baby book of the usual highlights – stump of the umbilical cord, first haircut cuttings, first words, when they start walking, etc. Sometimes I just write about general progress and attitudes. I have handmade paper books for my first two, and I often include writings and photos. For my son, I use a standard sort of memory book to include writings and photos as well as the more bulky things noted above."

–KATE HALLBERG

"I love keeping a journal for our son. I did one for his first year and then started his second year journal in a nice calendar of Van Gogh's paintings (which our son loves!)."

–MONIQUE RIVERA-ROGERS

"My former boss gave my son a baby time capsule from The Time Capsule Company. It is an aluminum canister that can be decorated and filled with baby's cherished keepsakes. I put one gift (stuffed toy, book, outfit, letter, etc.) from each of my son's relatives into the time capsule. We sealed the time capsule when he turned one, and will not open it until his 21st birthday. What makes the baby time capsule extra special is he will have keepsakes from relatives who are no longer living."

–SYLVIA ANDERSON

"I am having my daughter's first binky bronzed so we can give it to her. We are going to hang it on our Christmas tree every year, and then when she is older, we will let her keep it."

–SUSAN DOBRATZ

"I received an Olympus C-3020 digital camera for Christmas, one month after Sabine was born. I love this method because I can take as many pictures as I like, save them on my computer, alter them, print scrapbook pages with the pictures already on them, blow them up, shrink them down and upload them to various web sites (PhotoWorks.com, Snapfish.com). Not only can other people easily see them, but they can order their own reprints, and I can show off from any computer at work!"

–MICHELLE GEBHARD, D.O.

"I sew, so I kept all of my favorite/memorable outfits and made them into a baby memory quilt. I sewed the outfits onto a blanket that was special. When she gets into her "big girl" bed, it will be her quilt. I think I will save it for her when she grows out of it and give it back to her on her wedding day. I also have a 'time box' with newspapers and magazines from the day/month she was born. She will be able to look back and see what was going on when she was born. I do the baby book, photos, first lock of hair thing as well."

–GENEVIEVE MOLLOY

Pictures

Of course you'll take tons of pictures of your sweet angel yourself at home (and at the park, in the high chair, in the bath, etc.), and now with digital cameras, it's easier than ever to make high-quality prints in a wide variety of sizes. But we don't all own digital cameras yet, and sometimes, we just like the idea of getting pictures taken at a studio.

OUR FAVORITE PLACE TO GET BABY PICTURES TAKEN

Sears Portrait Studios

WHY WE LOVE IT

"I like Sears because the prices are great, and the picture packet is simply wonderful — so many pictures to both keep and give away. I can't get a deal like that anywhere else. It's definitely worth it to join their SmileSaversPlan®. And they have a variety of backgrounds and props."

–ELIZA LO CHIN, M.D.

"I get great coupons in the mail, and I'm part of their SmileSaversPlan, so I have no sitting fee for two years!"

–NINA MCCANN

"I really like Sears. It's inexpensive, plus they have a digital camera that allows you to view the pictures before buying them. The downside is having to wait three weeks for the pictures."

–HANNAH CHOW, M.D.

"I just like how they are really good with kids, and their picture quality is great. You also get to pick which photo you want to use for the package, and they keep taking pictures until you get the one that you like. I also like how they have cheap package deals, and they also have the SmileSaversPlan, where you do not pay for any sitting fees for two years. It's really great. And their workers are also very polite."

—ANGELA ALBRIGHT

"They offer a SmileSaversPlan where I pay $20 or so, and have no sitting fees for two years, plus the photographers are great. I have gone there since he was born and have never had a bad picture!"

—HEATHER HENDRICKSON

"The prices are inexpensive. The studios are clean, and the staff is friendly and good at their jobs — and the studios get the photos back in a timely manner."

—VALERIE VICARS DOWNS

"I take a lot of photos at home, and once a year, I take all the children to Sears for portraits. I like that I can see the pictures as they are taken. There is no second-guessing, wondering if the photo captured the baby in a good pose or a bad one."

—LISA BITTAR

"They dress your baby up in these cute costumes, and most of the time, you get your 8 x 10 free."

—AMANDA MARBREY

"I love the coupons! I can get her photos done once a month during this first year, and it never costs very much, and I always have more photos than I need!"

—HEATHER MEININGER

CHAPTER 6:

Food and Nutrition

Breast milk or formula is by far the most important source of nutrition for a baby during the first year. But sometime between four and six months, you'll probably introduce solids. And not long after that, it'll be table food, and before you know it, your toddler will be chowing down on spaghetti and macaroni and cheese. Here are our best tips for navigating the wonderful world of food with baby.

Baby Food

If you want to save money on baby food, and/or you really want to be sure there are only healthy ingredients in your baby's food, consider making your own. You can simply mash the food you're eating or use a food processor or blender to puree soft fruits and vegetables, and store them in ice cube trays. Just thaw, warm a little, and serve.

OUR TOP CHOICES

1. Gerber
2. Homemade
3. Organic — e.g., Gerber Tender Harvest ™, Earth's Best, Healthy Times, President's Choice (in Canada)

WHY WE LOVE THEM

"I like Gerber. They are one of the original baby food companies, and I trust their quality."

–COLLEEN GRACE WEAVER

"I prefer Gerber because of the selection and the food they have for different stages of babyhood. I also like the finger foods they offer for toddlers."

–DONNA DAVIDSON

"I love Gerber Tender Harvest because it contains less sugar and has tons of flavors for baby to try."

–LORI DRAGONETTI

"I prefer Gerber. It's a name that has been trusted for many years. I also prefer this brand because they have a wonderful selection of different foods in stages 1, 2, 3, toddler foods and finger foods. This brand doesn't taste or smell bad, and infants and toddlers really enjoy it."

–JESSICA GANE

"Right now, Noah is eating Gerber organics (Tender Harvest). I really like this food and the way it tastes. My philosophy on baby food is if I won't eat it, there is no way I will expect Noah to eat it. It is completely organic with no GMOs."

–DANA A. CROY

"One of the tastiest baby foods is Gerber's Tender Harvest, so even when your baby refuses to eat other brands of baby food, it's worth trying this one. It's also organically grown."

–ELIZA LO CHIN, M.D.

"I make my own by either boiling potatoes for mashed potatoes or mashing any of my food (besides meat) and feeding baby that. I would also make oatmeal and grits. Just anything that would be able to be mashed and easy to digest."

–LEAH CHEW

"I don't buy pre-made baby food. It's sooo easy and inexpensive to buy whole fruits, veggies, rice, oatmeal, etc. You cook, blend and serve. I store extra food in an ice cube tray in the freezer. One cube is the perfect serving size."

–SALLY FARRINGTON

"Homemade is easier, cheaper, healthier and tastes better. Simply steam veggies well and mash. With fruit, simply wait 'til it is very ripe, and mash or blend in a coffee grinder."

–MEGAN MILES

"I prefer to make my own. This way, I know where the food has been and exactly what is going into my child."

–ANITA GOOD

"I have started giving my baby President's Choice organic food found in Canada at most grocery stores at 69 cents a jar. I like that it's not full of pesticides and junk that she doesn't need. She loves it too!"

–CHANTAL LAURIN

"We liked Earth's Best because it is organic and had the best taste of all the baby foods we sampled (yes, we tasted them ourselves)! We also liked Healthy Times, but it was more difficult to find in stores."

–MICHELE LONGENBACH

Finger Foods

The most important thing we look for in first finger foods is safety. We don't want any potential choking hazards, which means foods like nuts, raisins, grapes and hot dogs are off limits for babies until at least age three.

We want our babies to get off to a healthy start, so we look for foods that are not only easy to gum, but are good for them, too. And we gravitate towards foods that are easy to make, easy to take with us when we go out and easy to clean up.

OUR NUMBER ONE FAVORITE FIRST FINGER FOOD

Cheerios®

WHY WE LOVE THEM

"Cheerios without a doubt! Cheerios can be broken in half and don't pose a severe choking hazard. They are low fat and full of good stuff for babies. They are a low-maintenance snack. You can take them anywhere with you, and they don't make a mess on the floor, in the car or on baby's hands, mouth or clothes."

–SHELLY SOLOMON HUGGINS

"Our favorite is the old standby: Cheerios. There must be something in the human genetic code that predisposes kids to love these things."

–SARAH PLETCHER

"They're easy to keep in your purse. Plus, they have nutritional value, dissolve easily in a little one's mouth and have a nice shape that works fine motor skills."

–KAREN HAAS

"My favorite first finger food for baby is Cheerios! They melt quickly in baby's mouth, they are low in sugar, and I never mind when Madyson wants to feed me them as well."

–LISA BITTAR

"Cheerios make a great first finger food. They help with hand-eye coordination, and my kids loved them."

–DANIELLE MARION-DOYLE

"Cheerios are the best first finger food to establish a healthy eating habit. They taste good, melt in milk readily and are easy to store, carry and serve. My daughter used to stick her little fingers through the holes of moistened Cheerios and make fingertip rings. She would then eat them off her fingers with relish."

–SUSAN LONERGAN

"Cheerios have been my favorite with my boys, mainly because you can break them in half, which almost eliminates any chance of them choking, and they are easily mushed by the baby when they have only a few teeth."

–BROOKE ULINSKI

"They are easy to pick up, provide nutrients, fun for kids to stack and play with, and there is little chance of an unexpected allergy if you have introduced other grain products, such as [baby] cereals."

–REBECCA CURTIS

"There isn't a lot of sugar in them, and they are the right size for small fingers. They also get really soggy quickly, so there is not much of a choking hazard."

–DENINE SCALLEN

"My son loves Cheerios, and so do I. They are so easy to pick up, and they dissolve a bit in his mouth, so they are easy to swallow. Plus, they don't slip and slide like fruit. They do have a bit of sugar, but it's not as bad as the baby biscuits."

–CARA VINCENS

"They are easy to eat and easy to clean up when the inevitable gravity experiments start."

–DEBBIE PALMER

"Cheerios are my favorite because you can simply throw them in a zipper-lock bag and always have them on hand in the diaper bag."

–REBECCA HARPER

"They are great for pincher-finger dexterity development; they present a minimal choking hazard (there's a hole in them and they melt in your mouth if not chewed), are easily transportable and will not rot."

–SIDNEY MARKS

"They are small, tasty and less of a choking hazard than other foods because they will dissolve in saliva."

–JENNIFER ROSE

"They are healthy, and babies just love them."

–DEBBY MADRID

Healthy Snacks

We know that snacks are important to kids' diets, so we want them to be as satisfying and nutritious as possible. Here are our favorites.

THE FIVE SNACKS WE FEEL BEST ABOUT GIVING OUR KIDS

1. Fruit
2. Vegetables with or without dip
3. Yogurt
4. Peanut butter and...apple slices, bananas, celery
5. Cheese

WHY WE LOVE THEM

"My son always liked sliced apples with a little peanut butter on them. A very healthy snack and very tasty. It was also a big hit at the day care where I worked."

–VERONICA WILSON

"My favorite healthy snack for kids is fruit. When they were infants, they had applesauce. As older kids, I peel and slice apples, pears, peel oranges, wash blueberries, slice strawberries, etc. This family of four goes through five apples, five pears, one bunch of bananas and usually one or

two containers of blueberries, strawberries, cherries or whatever is in season every week. Then I don't feel so bad if they don't eat their vegetables."

–MICHELE F. CARLON, M.D.

"We keep serving size fruit on hand. You can freeze it too, to make sure there's always a snack ready. Yogurt is also really good for those little ones who like to dip."

–BRENDA BROWN

"Grapes, strawberries and other fresh fruit are my favorite healthy snack. Sometimes I put strawberries over vanilla yogurt for a special treat."

–JENNIFER YOUNG

"Bananas with anything — peanut butter or a smoothie. Kids love smoothies because it is the healthy version of a milkshake. They think they're getting a huge treat."

–MARI KISTLER

"Fruit, fruit and more fruit! It has excellent vitamins and fiber, plus natural sugars for an extra energy boost. My son helps pick out fresh fruit at the grocery store. We have a deal that he will try some of every type of fruit he chooses and he usually enjoys them all."

–SYLVIA ANDERSON

"My kids love baby carrots, apples, bananas and cantaloupe."

–DANIELLE MARION-DOYLE

"We blanch carrot sticks to make them easier to chew. Blanching softens them and brings out more natural sweetness. Then we chill them for a little crispness and also to make them friendly to tender gums. We also go through a lot of sliced cheese."

–DEBBIE PALMER

"Kids love a cup of frozen peas! On a warm day, they are refreshing and a lot healthier than ice cream."

–CARA VINCENS

"We try to have him only eat healthy snacks, but I must say that Gardenburger veggie patties have some great stuff in them (brown rice, tomatoes, celery, onions, etc.) all in one sitting."

MONIQUE RIVERA-ROGERS

"Once they are old enough, trays of fruits and veggies with a little dip work wonders. My kids love anything they can grab and eat, and the dip is a little something extra."

–BROOKE ULINSKI

"My kids like ants on a log. It's celery with peanut butter down the middle and topped with raisins. Sounds gross, but it's delicious."

–ERIKA PLODZIEN

"I like Go-Gurt (yogurt in a tube). It's easy, filling, provides calcium and is nutritious. It's also great for babies and eliminates the need for utensils."

–ELIZA LO CHIN, M.D.

"String cheese is not messy, and it's convenient. One stick is usually a good portion for a child. Yogurt is another favorite, as are raw carrots and dip, sliced fruit, such as grapes and watermelon or sliced turkey."

–DIANE BEDROSIAN, M.D.

"My preschool son and toddler daughter love single-serving cheese sticks, dried fruit (raisins, dried pears, dried apricots, prunes, etc.) and frozen mixed vegetables (served frozen)."

–SIDNEY MARKS

Vegetables

Lots of kids, especially babies and toddlers, like vegetables — probably because they haven't been exposed to a lot of sugary, processed foods yet. But many don't like vegetables at all, which can become a bigger problem as they get older and enter the "picky eater" stage. Here are our best recommendations for coping with vegetable-averse kids

✓ Serve with dip.

"Offer veggies raw or slightly steamed (no seasoning) and a variety of dips – even ketchup can make the pickiest of eaters love broccoli."

–LYNN PARKS

"Kids love to dip, so I think giving them various dipping sauces – ketchup, ranch dressing, barbecue sauce or cheese – encourages them to eat vegetables."

–HOLLY COCCHIOLA

✓ Cover them with cheese.

"Cheese works. Kids will eat almost anything if it has cheese on it."
                                                            –BROOKE KUHNS

✓ Hide them in pasta sauces and other foods they like.

"I made a pasta sauce and puree vegetables and put that in the sauce."
                                                            –ANN STOWE

"Hide them in casseroles and soups. Also, I got my kids to eat carrot sticks when I made little faces with their lunches and used carrots as stick-up hair."
                                                            –TRACY PRITCHARD

"My son hates vegetables. I have to be very sneaky to get him to eat them. At our house, the easiest way is to add them directly to whatever food we are serving. For example, add mushrooms and black olives to spaghetti sauce, green beans to just about any casserole, corn to spicy pasta salads or broccoli to creamy soups."
                                                            –SYLVIA ANDERSON

"One of my favorite ways to get the kids to eat vegetables is to put them in their favorite foods. I shred zucchini and carrots into meatloaf (and I use oatmeal instead of bread crumbs as the filler) and put broccoli into macaroni and cheese. My Ellie LOVES asparagus, and I don't have to hide it anywhere. In fact, if I want any myself, I need to hide it from her! Spaghetti sauce is another favorite place to hide vegetables."
                                                            –MICHELE F. CARLON, M.D.

"I sneak carrots and zucchini into all of my pancakes and muffins. I also use finely-chopped spinach in lots of stuff. If it is spread out with chicken and pasta, they don't even realize they are eating it."
                                                            –PATRICIA ARNOLD

"My kids like vegetables, but I still have some tricks up my sleeve to sneak more in. One idea is making zucchini or pumpkin muffins using part whole wheat pastry flour and decreasing the sugar. Even though my kids are past the baby food stage, I still keep a couple of jars of pureed vegetables on hand to add to other foods. I add carrots to anything with a tomato base (such as ravioli or spaghetti). I also add green beans or carrots to macaroni and cheese. The kids don't know they're eating extra

vegetables. They also enjoy eating raw carrots with dip or celery with peanut butter and raisins."

–JULIE BARTLETT

✓ **Eat them yourself, and offer them over and over again without judging the response.**

"Our kids love vegetables. We've always been very positive about them and never told them vegetables are yucky (except their daddy with peas, but we've overcome that). We eat a lot of vegetables, both cooked and raw, and they see that. They taste everything, and usually find that they like it. If they don't like something, we just offer it again at a different meal without making a fuss. Repeat exposure often does the trick."

–DEBBIE PALMER

"Continual introduction works. After five times, they usually like it."

–JENNIFER ROSE

"I try to remember that children may need to try a new food five-to-ten times before they develop a taste for it. Most importantly, make sure eating is not a battle. The more you push a child to eat a food they don't like, the more they will resist. Children will naturally balance their own diet when presented with healthy choices. Putting pressure on kids to eat certain foods or making other foods off limits just sets them up for food issues later."

–MEGAN MILES

✓ **Serve them first before the rest of the meal.**

"My best discovery is the PuPu platter – a large platter with seven sections. I put a different cut-up fruit and vegetable in each section and put it on the table when the kids are watching TV before dinner. The snack disappears in minutes, and the kids love it without realizing they're eating something healthy. Then, because they've had their fruits and veggies, I don't need to stress out about trying to get them to eat veggies at dinner. And it takes care of the pre-dinner irritability."

–DONNICA L. MOORE, M.D.

"I started giving my twins their veggies prior to any other part of the meal. I would place it on their trays, and they were probably thinking it was all they were getting. I started this practice when they started eating *finger foods. I continue it today, and veggies are still a big hit. It has become a big joke that my kids eat green beans as a snack."*

–LORI VANCE

✓ Don't force the issue, and make all foods equal.

"I don't make a big deal out of MUST finishing veggies before dessert from the beginning. It should be that all food is equal. Dessert should not be on a higher level than the main course."

–REBECCA CURTIS

"A great piece of advice as far as food and kids: Your responsibility as the parent is to put healthy food in front of the child, and the child's responsibility is to eat the food. I have tried not to overextend myself too much as far as talking my son into eating this or making him eat that...most kids need to see a food several times (and often completely reject it several times) before it becomes familiar enough that they eat it or try it. You would be amazed at how this is true: You just look up one day, and they are eating something they wouldn't even look at the first several times.

"If you keep the stigma and tension off healthy foods (veggies, etc.) by not trying to sell them, but just consistently offering them, the kids will just naturally eat them. If you went to a restaurant, and someone was really working hard to get you to eat something, wouldn't you be suspicious?"

–SARAH PLETCHER

CHAPTER 7:

Sickness and Health

If you're lucky, the only health-related issue you'll face the first year is teething. More likely, you'll have at least one cold or ear infection, though. Don't fret. We're here with our best tips and tricks to get through it.

Teething

It's not exactly an illness, but it might as well be for some babies. Not only do they drool like crazy and chew on anything and everything in sight, but they can become cranky, feverish, restless (read: up all night) and even develop cold symptoms. Here are our best strategies for coping.

THE EIGHT BEST WAYS TO RELIEVE TEETHING PAIN

1. Teething rings
2. Cold or frozen washcloth
3. Tylenol® or Motrin®
4. Orajel®
5. Hyland's Teething Tablets
6. Frozen bagels or waffles to chew on
7. Popsicles®
8. Baby Safe Feeder

WHY WE RECOMMEND THEM

"I use a warm teething ring or a warm baby wash cloth to compress lightly on the gums."

–DAWN KIRNON, M.D.

"I used the iced teething rings a lot, but also gave them Tylenol if they were clearly uncomfortable."

–DONNICA L. MOORE, M.D.

"Teething rings from the freezer are okay, but they don't last that long and they aren't exactly the easiest thing for a little baby to handle, especially if they are still young where they can't hold it. So my remedy is a cold, damp washcloth. My son bites it and sucks on it, and he can crawl around with it hanging from his mouth. It's also a lot quicker than waiting for a ring to get chilly because some cold water is all it takes. Great in the summer, too, because you can wipe him down with it first or lay it on his belly while he bites it."

–ANITA GOOD

"My daughter likes cold carrots and teething rings. I also give her Motrin for the pain."

–JESSICA GANE

"Hyland's Teething Tablets are amazing. I wish I had known about them with my oldest son."

–DENINE SCALLEN.

"Frozen mini bagels, a frozen wash cloth or their favorite – your finger (washed thoroughly first)."

–MICHELLE GEBHARD, D.O.

"Hyland's Teething Tablets and Hyland's Teething Gel work very well. I have found they seem to work better than Baby Orajel®. Also, a cold, wet, baby washcloth given to a baby to suck/teethe on seems to help."

–DIANE BEDROSIAN, M.D

"My sons loved chewing on a frozen bagel when they were trying to cut teeth. It was sort of soft and tasted a lot better than a plastic ring."

–LORI STUSSIE

"I found ice pops work great for my kids. They love the way they taste, and they help numb their gums at the same time. There is also a thing you can get at the store called a Baby Safe Feeder that can hold fruit and ice cubes and things they would not normally be able to eat. With this, they can chew on these foods, but can't choke on them. It has a handle so they can hold it themselves. My son seemed to go through them pretty quickly, but I thought they were well worth it."

–BROOKE ULINSKI

"I discovered the Baby Safe Feeder after trying everything else first. I just put cut-up apple, pear, cantaloupe, whatever, in there, and he just *bites away. It is a big drool-yielder, but well worth it, as I know it provided the best relief out of anything else we tried."*

—BETH MILLER

When They Get Sick

Nothing is more heartbreaking than seeing your innocent babe get sick. They can't sleep; they can't eat; they just lose all of their spunk. Fortunately, first babies usually get sick less frequently than subsequent children, and by the time you have your second (or third, fourth, fifth...), you'll have been through it all. Here are our best ideas for coping when baby isn't feeling quite up to snuff.

TAKING BABY'S TEMPERATURE

In general, we like using the ear thermometer for quick readings. It's fast, non-invasive and if you know how to use an ear thermometer well, we've found it's great.

Unfortunately, we're not all experts at using the ear thermometer, which means readings can vary widely, depending on the shape of the child's eardrum and the angle at which you insert the thermometer into the child's ear. Moreover, ear thermometers are expensive. Other alternatives for quick readings include the pacifier thermometer and strips across the forehead.

No matter what method you use, you have to know how to do it right. All methods, including rectal, can register an inaccurate temperature if they aren't done correctly.

OUR FAVORITE METHOD

Under the Arm

WHY WE LIKE IT

"Under the arm is much less invasive than the rectal method and cheaper than the ear thermometer."

—COLLEEN GRACE WEAVER

"I prefer to take my baby's temperature using the underarm method. It is not as intrusive as the rectal or the ear, which tends to have the babies

squirming/tense from the unfamiliar feeling of a thermometer being inserted into their bodies."

–DAWN KIRNON, M.D.

"I prefer to take my daughter's temperature under her arm. This way, I can get the temperature I need to get, and I can comfort her at the same time."

–JESSICA GANE

"I like the underarm method because it gives me an excuse to cuddle my child."

–SARA DIXON

"I like the under-the-arm thermometer because I am holding my sick child, so she feels comforted. It is an inexpensive thermometer, and it gives you an accurate reading."

–PATRICIA ARNOLD

"First the ear, then if it's high, I double check under the arm. The ear is quick, and under the arm is very accurate."

–SABRINA LANE

"I prefer taking the temperature under the arm (axillary). This method tends to be better tolerated by babies, while being fairly accurate. Ear thermometers, despite product literature to the contrary, really are not very reliable under the age of 6 months, or at very high temperatures. We do not use them at all in our office for babies under 6 months, and if there is a question of high fever in older kids, we will often take an axillary or rectal temperature just to be sure the ear reading is accurate. Most of the time, if you leave the thermometer under the arm long enough, the reading will be reliable, but if you feel the reading does not correlate with how your child feels, you can always double-check by measuring a rectal temperature."

–DIANE BEDROSIAN, M.D.

"I would have to say I like the new Vicks ® underarm sticker wearable/disposable thermometer. It sticks to the baby's underarm and can be read all day long. The ear thermometers don't seem to give an accurate reading because the ear canal is too narrow to accommodate the part of the thermometer that goes into the ear. With the underarm thermometer, if I suspect my daughter has a temperature, I can stick one on and leave it there, and read it multiple times throughout the day, so I can see if the medicine is bringing the temperature down."

–KAREN HURST

When Baby Has a Cold

Most doctors don't recommend giving very young babies cold medicines. That means you have to resort to mom-tested comfort strategies. Here are our favorites.

Our Five Favorite Cold Remedies

1. Sit in a steamy shower.
2. Give baby a warm bath with a children's vapor bath product or a rubdown with a children's vapor cream, such as Johnson's Soothing Vapor Cream® or Soothing Vapor Bath®
3. Give baby plenty of rest, fluids and your tender loving care.
4. Use saline nasal drops.
5. Use a vaporizer.

"Turning the shower on hot and sitting in the bathroom lets the steam relieve congestion. Menthol baby baths and a cool mist humidifier also do the trick."

–Becky Gaston

"I like bringing the baby into a steamy bathroom after taking a hot shower. I get the relaxation of the shower, and she gets the nasal clearance that only steam seems to accomplish. It helps if I allow the water to continually run after bringing her in there. All natural and no adverse effects."

–Caren Sadikman, M.D.

"A good old-fashioned steam bath is always my favorite. We just run the hot water shower and sit in the bathroom for 15 minutes at a time. The steam really helps clear out nasal passages and loosens chest congestion. Mom/Dad gets a spa treatment at the same time!"

–Staci Paro

"I like Tylenol Cold and Johnson's® Soothing Vapor Cream and Soothing Vapor Bath because they are easily administered, they don't make the problem worse and they help my son feel better faster."

–Valerie Vicars Downs

"I love Johnson's Soothing Vapor Bath and Soothing Vapor Cream to soothe a baby with a cold. I'll try these first before resorting to medicines.

The vaporizing bath clears those stuffed up nasal passages so well and calms a fussy, sick baby."

–STEPHANIE MARTIN

"I recommend rest (to let the body heal), fluids to re-hydrate the body and lots of love (who doesn't like that anytime)?"

–HOLLY COCCHIOLA

"If there is just a runny nose, I use a saline nose spray. I try to stay as natural as possible."

–BARBARA NICHOLS

"I don't like to give my kids cold medicine if I can help it, especially when they're babies. And at any rate, I've found that nothing in a bottle beats some Little Noses® saline drops, a nasal aspirator and some Johnson's Soothing Vapor Bath."

–BROOKE KUHNS

"I use homemade nasal drops: one-fourth teaspoon of salt plus eight ounces of boiled water, cooled completely."

–SABRINA LANE

"As soon as they start with the sniffles, I pull out a cool air vaporizer."

–BROOKE ULINSKI

OUR FAVORITE PAIN-RELIEVER/FEVER-REDUCER

Tylenol®

WHY WE RECOMMEND IT

"I like Tylenol because it works quickly and my kids always liked the taste."

–DONNICA L. MOORE, M.D.

"Tylenol has always been a favorite because it seems to work better than anything else."

–VERONICA WILSON

"Tylenol, Tylenol, Tylenol. It doesn't interfere with almost any other medication, and it doesn't have any side effects. I feel safe using it, which is very important to a new mom!"

–STACI PARO

"I use Tylenol first because it has a long track record of safety in children, but for the very high temperatures or persistent temperatures, I use Motrin or Advil because it seems to be more effective."

–ELIZA LO CHIN, M.D.

"I like Tylenol for infants because it tastes the best and works. But if my daughter has a fever for over 24 hours, then I alternate between Tylenol and Motrin."

–ERIKA PLODZIEN

GETTING THEM TO TAKE MEDICINE

With all the fun flavors medicine comes in nowadays (grape, cherry, bubble gum, etc.), you'd think babies would love taking it. After all, it has to taste better than rice cereal, right? But some babies are tough customers when it comes to taking any kind of medicine, no matter how good it's supposed to taste. Try these ideas when your little one is fighting you every step of the way.

THE THREE BEST WAYS TO GIVE A SQUIRMY BABY MEDICINE

1. Squirt it into the baby's cheek.
2. Mix it with something they like.
3. Make it fun.

"Hold at an upright angle and squirt the medicine with a dropper toward the back of the child's inner cheek."

–SARA DIXON

"I always put them in their seat or in the high chair, reclined, but not laying down, and I squirt some in the back corner of the cheek and put their pacifier in their mouth right away. So even if the medicine is really yucky, they know and have an attachment to the pacifier, so they are going to suck on it, and presto, the medicine is down before they know what happened."

–BROOKE KUHNS

"I would put it in a dropper and squeeze the medicine down the side of the baby's mouth (along the inside of the cheek) and then blow into the baby's

face to make her swallow. A pharmacist recommended putting the medicine in grape juice or chocolate milk. He explained that these two substances will mask most bad-tasting medicines. I tried this a couple of times, but you have to be careful to make sure the baby drinks all of it. Also, always check with a pharmacist before mixing medicine with anything."

–JULIE BARTLETT

"I found that mixing with one tablespoon of juice, pudding or Jello® (whatever is their favorite) along with the meds was always magic. You don't have to worry about them not finishing because it's a small amount compared to mixing it in a cup of juice."

–BOBBI ANNAL

"In the Emergency Room, we have tried them all. I tend to give them something they like, then give them the medicine with the same voice (mmm...cherries). Otherwise, crush the pill form into applesauce or pudding (butterscotch works best actually) and make it seem like a treat because they are sick. For really young babies, shoot it towards the back of the mouth with a syringe a little at a time and chase it with some juice or milk that they like to drink."

–MICHELLE GEBHARD, D.O.

"We make a big deal out of it in our house. When it's time to take it for the first time, we make it seem exciting, almost like she is getting an extra special treat. We treat it like she is getting an extended dessert. I swear the last time she was on Amoxicillin, she got excited every time she saw the medicine bottle. We've never had a difficult time with her taking medicine."

–DONNA DAVIDSON

"We pretend Daddy's taking it."

–NINA MCCANN

"Try using funny/silly tricks to get a baby to take the medicine by singing 'Ah...' with your mouth wide open to model it for the baby. Sing so that the baby can feel free to sing too, then gently place the medicine in the mouth."

–DAWN KIRNON, M.D.

"I get my husband to help me to play games with our kids. We've used funny faces, expressions and voices. When they forget that medicine is with us, and we see their mouths open, we quickly put the medicine in their mouths."

–CONNIE CHOATE

GETTING A GOOD NIGHT'S REST WHEN THEY ARE SICK

Nighttime is the worst time for little ones when they're sick. Illnesses seem to get worse at night, and it's hard to sleep when you're all stuffed up. Here's what we do to help them sleep at night and feel better overall.

THE FIVE BEST WAYS TO HELP A SICK BABY SLEEP

1. Give lots of tender loving care.
2. Use a soothing children's vapor lotion or vapor bath product, such as Johnson's Soothing Vapor Cream® or Soothing Vapor Bath®
3. Elevate the baby's head.
4. Sleep with baby or let them fall asleep on you.
5. Use a vaporizer.

"Holding them close to you makes them feel a lot better. You wouldn't believe how much a mommy's love can help a cold."

–AMANDA MARBREY

"I usually bring them out in the living room with me, and we 'camp' on the couch or recliner."

–KELI LOVELAND

"I offer just old-fashioned TLC – lots of holding and hugging, fresh air and playing any of her favorite games for distraction."

–CAREN SADIKMAN, M.D.

"I cuddle them with me and read plenty of stories."

–BOBBI ANNAL

"I rub their backs and sing them to sleep."

–DONNICA L. MOORE, M.D.

"Give the child a rubdown with soothing lotion, tell them a story and stay with them till they fall asleep."

–LAMIEL OESTERREICHER

"Roll up a towel and put it under his mattress at the head of the bed to help relieve nasal congestion."

–KATHLEEN CONROY

"Letting small ones sleep in a car seat or carrier lets them breathe better."

–VERONICA WILSON

"Co-sleeping is a lifesaver when little ones are sick. Nothing is more comforting than to cuddle up with Mommy or Daddy when they are not feeling well. This has the added benefit of being right there if they get sicker during the night."

–MEGAN MILES

"I would rock my children to sleep or let them lay down with me in my bed when they were sick or couldn't sleep. I also would sometimes give them a little massage with some oil."

–BRENDA DINTIMAN, M.D.

"I give them a nice warm bath, then nurse until they fall asleep. When my babies are little, I sleep with them in the rocker to help keep their heads elevated, so they don't choke. Also, I can feel if a fever breaks out."

–BARBARA NICHOLS

"The humidifier has been a great help with this. Not only does the moisture help, but it has a sound that lulls them to sleep."

–WENDY DOUGLAS

BRUSHING TEETH

We believe that earlier is better when it comes to teaching proper dental hygiene. Even if your baby has only one or two teeth, you can begin practicing br ushing. When your child is older, squirmier and potentially more defiant, here are our favorite tricks.

THE TOP FIVE WAYS TO GET KIDS TO BRUSH THEIR TEETH

1. Brush together.
2. Give them fun toothbrushes.
3. Buy toothpaste that tastes good.
4. Make it part of your daily routine.
5. Sing a tooth-brushing song.

"Liam is a copycat, so we get him to brush his teeth by sitting him on the counter while we brush our teeth. He loves to do anything we do. We do have to help him make sure he gets them all brushed well, but he doesn't seem to mind since he's participating in the same activity we are."

–HEATHER FRENCH

"I let her brush my teeth if she lets me brush hers...then I let her brush her teeth by herself."

–CHELSEA COFFEY HAMMAN

"I show Nevey how to brush her teeth by brushing my teeth first and making it look fun and easy. I just talk her through it and explain to her what I am doing. She then seems to cooperate better."

–JODI STEGER

"I have my 19-month-old brush her teeth with me, and we brush together right before bed. Then we tuck her in and tell her a story."

–CRYSTAL SHOULTS

"I get them cool toothbrushes. My boys have Spiderman and Bob the Builder® toothbrushes and Buzz Lightyear toothpaste, so they do it without my even having to ask."

–BROOKE ULINSKI

"I play the zoo game with my kids. I tell them I can see alligators, elephants and zebras in their mouths, and then we try to brush them away. This has always gotten a huge giggle out of them, and they let me spend more time brushing each tooth."

–STEPHANIE R. SMITH

"Brushing teeth is a part of our evening routine. Each child has mommy brush their teeth, while mommy sings them a song. Then mommy hands

them the toothbrush, and they get to try it on their own. We do this right before night-night stories and bed."

–Theresa Smead

"First of all, find a toothbrush and toothpaste with their favorite character. Let them play with the toothbrush. We would take turns. I would let my daughter play and chew on the brush, then when it was my turn, I would brush her teeth."

–Michelle Laney

"Sing a song! Barney has a great song for teeth-brushing and of course, you can always make up your own. We also take turns brushing our daughter's teeth, then give her a chance to brush her teddy bear's teeth...it makes it seem more fun."

Jennifer Young

"We have our daughter brush hers when we brush ours. We play a game and sing a song, 'This is the way we brush our teeth, brush our teeth, this is the way we brush our teeth so we can get them clean.' My daughter loves it."

–Debby Madrid

CHAPTER 8:

Entertainment

We don't think you need to spend a lot of money to play with your baby. Many of the most exciting and stimulating "toys" for babies are plain old household objects, such as measuring cups (great for stacking), pots and pans (what baby doesn't love to make noise?), your keys and everyone's favorite, the remote control. Of course, you may not want your baby teething on your car keys or your remote control, but we're just talking about what they'd *want* to play with here, not what you'd *let* them play with.

Toys

When we're shopping for toys, safety is critical – that means no small parts, long cords or strings that can be wrapped around baby's neck. We also look for toys that are durable, colorful and engaging.

OUR NUMBER ONE FAVORITE FIRST TOY FOR BABY

Activity Arch/Baby Gym

WHY WE LOVE IT

"My baby is only 4 months old. So far, his favorite toy is a kick and sound gym. It has the bar at the bottom, and when he kicks it, it plays music and makes lights. It also has the toys that hang down from the top part. He really enjoys this. I can lay him on the floor, and he'll play with it forever."

–BRANDY CHARLES

"We had an arch gym play mat that Neve would sit under for long periods and stare at the toys dangling above her, then it was great to watch her develop her ability to reach and then bat at the toys. She also loved the kick-gym. She would just go nuts kicking and watching as she made the toys turn above her head."

–JODI STEGER

"One of our favorite first toys was the Gymini®, which a baby lies under and can touch/kick all the toys hanging down. It's black, white and red and really keeps them entertained."

–SHARON LICHTENFELD

"The Gymini is great for keeping baby entertained for short spans of time. Sometimes, she would even fall asleep under it!"

–STACEY SKLAR

OUR TOP THREE FAVORITE BRANDS OF BABY TOYS

1. Fisher-Price®
2. Sassy®
3. Lamaze

WHY WE LOVE THEM

"Fisher-Price just seems to know what fascinates children, and they last forever."

–DEBORAH THERIAULT

"I absolutely love everything by Fisher-Price. They are accurate in their age ranges and have the most vibrant colors and characters."

–ANNA MARIA JOHNSON

"My favorites have been Lamaze and Sassy toys. They're creative, very safe, colorful and stimulating. For example, just when my daughter loved to shake things, there was a Lamaze toy with multiple handles for shaking, designed for her age group. Now she likes pulling things on strings, so I got her the Lamaze cars on a string that attach to each other with velcro."

–STACEY SKLAR

"I especially like the Sassy brand toys because they are eye-catching and designed to be age-appropriate. They are also quite durable."

–HANNAH CHOW, M.D.

"I love Fisher-Price toys. They are bright, colorful and very inexpensive. They are also very durable."

–KATE STEIMAN

"Sassy has such great rattles/toys for babies. They are bright in color, have noise and are easy for them to chew on without getting hurt."

–LORI VANCE

"I like Lamaze. The fabric washes well, and the toys are very educational ...putting things in and taking them out, stacking, sorting, etc."

–JENNIFER YOUNG

"Fisher-Price toys are so well made and so versatile."

–SABRINA LANE

"I love Sassy toys! They are fun, they let your child be creative, they are brightly colored, very strong and hold up against the poundings that my ten-month-old gives them – especially the bath toys. They are so wonderful I want to take them in the tub with me!"

–K. SCARLETT SHAW

"Sassy has nice bright colors, and they also have a good assortment of black, white and red toys."

–DIANNA SCHISSER

"Fisher-Price is a trustworthy brand. Their items are sturdy, inexpensive, colorful and reasonable for little ones. Especially because a lot of their stuff is LOW TECH. Research has shown that kids do better with toys that require and help them nurture their own creativity."

–SHELLY SOLOMON HUGGINS

"I like the Sassy toys for my infant, since they tend to really stimulate him, and my favorite for my toddler is Fisher-Price, since their toys are a little more appropriate for his age group."

–REBECCA HARPER

"I played with Little People® when I was a child and now my daughter is in love with them too. Fisher-Price has quality toys that are very hard to break...which is a good thing when you have a toddler."

–STEPHANIE HOSSZU

Books

What better way to bond with your baby, help him learn about the world or teach her language than by reading? Experts recommend reading to babies from birth.

1. *Goodnight Moon* by Margaret Wise Brown
2. Anything by Sandra Boynton, especially *The Going to Bed Book*
3. *Brown Bear, Brown Bear, What Do You See?* and other books by Eric Carle
4. *Good Night, Gorilla* by Peggy Rathmann
5. Anything by Dr. Seuss
6. *Guess How Much I Love You* by Sam McBratney
7. Board books with pictures of babies, such as *Baby Faces, I Am a Baby* and *Everywhere Babies*
8. *Pat the Bunny* books by Dorothy Kunhardt and Edith Kunhardt
9. *Time for Bed* by Mem Fox
10. *The Big Red Barn* by Margaret Wise Brown

WHY WE LOVE THEM

"Goodnight Moon *by Margaret Wise Brown is my favorite. I love the little story, and the illustrations in the book are so heart-warming."*

–LYNN PARKS

"Brown Bear, Brown Bear, What Do You See? *and* Goodnight Moon *have been my favorites for all three of my daughters. I like the rhyming with* Brown Bear *– my kids pick up on that real fast – and I always read* Goodnight Moon *before bed."*

–ELICIA MOORE

"Favorite first books include Good Night, Gorilla, *Pat the Bunny,* I Like it When... *and* Time for Bed. Good Night, Gorilla *is so wonderful because it is a story without words, allowing the parent to 'tell' the story to the child's age/stage of development. There is enough detail in the drawings to captivate a three-year-old's attention (look for the balloon as it flies up and away in the sky), and a basic enough story to appeal to younger kids.* Pat the Bunny *is a classic. It is wonderful because it is an interactive book, encouraging even the youngest to touch/look/smell. I like the fact that it includes a Daddy (Daddy's scratchy face).*

"I Like It When... *is a story of all the things a parent and young* penguin like to do together. Its very simple, vivid drawings depict every day activities that the parent and child share – eating new things, helping, dancing, splashing, hugging, etc. This is my very favorite book. Finally, Time for Bed is an incredibly good bedtime book. With nice rhymes and soft illustrations of parent/child animals, it creates a mood for sleep. The youngest readers will enjoy identifying the animals on each page. Older readers will learn the names for baby animals (calf, foal, fawn, etc.) and enjoy memorizing the rhymes. We give this book often as a baby present."

–SIDNEY MARKS

"We like Goodnight Moon and anything by Sandra Boynton. They are all board books, with fun pictures, an easy-to-follow story, they wipe clean, and my toddler LOVES them. He also adores Everywhere Babies by Susan Meyers. Wonderful pictures and a good rhyming story. Lots of babies doing lots of different things on their way to the first birthday."

–SHERYL MADDEN

"My absolute favorite baby book is Guess How Much I Love You by Sam McBratney. The love a parent has for a child is so evident and endearing in this book."

–DANIELLE MARION-DOYLE

"The Big Red Barn is one of our all-time favorites. We love the melodious text and the animal characters always seem to fascinate our children. After reading it many, many times, we had it committed to memory and could recite it out loud like a poem."

–SUSAN TACHNA

"Guess How Much I Love You is a favorite because it was fairly easy reading, meaning it held their attention, and you get to say 'I love you' a lot."

–TRACY PRITCHARD

"I like any books by Sandra Boynton. I like the sing-song style of the poems, and they are lots of fun to read and look at."

–LISA MCDONALD

"I like Goodnight Moon because it is very colorful and has a simple, flowing story that lulls a baby to sleep (and if not sleep, at least it tends to calm her down)."

–HEATHER MEININGER

"Our son's first book was One Fish, Two Fish, Red Fish, Blue Fish *by Dr. Seuss. I love the bright colors and drawings and the rhyming."*

–MICHELE LONGENBACH

"All of my children love The Foot Book *by Dr. Seuss. We began reading it to our first born when he was about six months old and have read it to our other children as well. We played with their feet while we read it, and they still love it. They are seven, six and three now."*

–KRISTEN MATH

"I really recommend My Many Colored Days *by Dr. Seuss. It teaches kids about emotions and that they're all okay to have, and it uses colors to describe them. It's Sam's favorite book."*

–BETH MILLER

"For toddlers, I absolute love Dr. Seuss books. They are fun, exciting and give you a chance to just be silly with your kids. I loved them when I was a child, and now I get to share them with my children!"

–K. SCARLETT SHAW

"My favorite first book for babies are any with baby faces in them (e.g., I Am a Baby*). Infants love looking at other infants, and older children enjoy identifying body parts and expressions."*

–HANNAH CHOW, M.D.

" I like Baby Faces. *My son loves to look at pictures of other babies."*

–KARI RYDELL

Music

OUR TOP FIVE FAVORITE MUSICAL ARTISTS/RECORDINGS FOR LITTLE ONES

1. Raffi
2. Wee Sing
3. The Wiggles
4. Baby Einstein series, including *Baby Mozart, Baby Beethoven, Baby Bach, Baby Vivaldi*, etc.
5. Veggie Tales

WHY WE LOVE THEM

"Any of the Wee Sing tapes are great. Our favorite is Children's Songs and Fingerplays, *since we can act out the words. The Wee Sing tapes are great refreshers if you haven't heard the songs since childhood."*

–KIMBERLY MERCURIO, M.D.

"I like the Veggie Tales tapes because they teach children morals through song."

–BARBARA EVANS

"I love the Raffi songs – nice beat and easy to sing along with."

–DIANNA SCHISSER

"I like The Wiggles Yummy Yummy *because the songs are different, upbeat and easy for little ones to learn the words to."*

–JENNIFER YOUNG

"Raffi is the first kiddie tape I listened to with my daughter when she was young, and she really responded to it. Eventually, we'd sing along together."

–ANN STOWE

Television and Videos

We know that kids this age don't need to watch television. But we're also realistic. Sometimes we need 15 minutes of uninterrupted time to get dinner on the table. When we do make the choice to allow our little ones to watch, though, we want to make sure that what they're watching is as beneficial to them as possible. We look for shows/videos that are educational and entertaining at the same time.

OUR TOP THREE FAVORITE TELEVISION SHOWS FOR LITTLE ONES

1. Sesame Street
2. Blue's Clues
3. Dora the Explorer

WHY WE LOVE THEM

"I love Sesame Street *and so does my daughter! It teaches good behavior, sounds, letters, numbers and has lots of humor for adults sprinkled in it."*

–STEPHANIE HOSSZU

"Nick, Jr. is hands down the best toddler/preschool television programming, especially Blue's Clues *and* Dora the Explorer. *The girls get very involved with the shows, jumping up and down, trying to find the clues or warn Dora about Swiper. Much better than just vegging out in front of the set."*

–JULIE WONDERLING

"My kids really like Blue's Clues. *They love interacting with the host and helping to find the clues and solve the mystery. I like it because the kids actually use their minds when they watch and get actively involved in solving the riddle."*

–JULIE BARTLETT

"I loved watching Sesame Street *even before I had kids, but now they really teach my daughter a lot, and she thinks it's all just fun."*

–SABRINA LANE

"My favorite TV show for toddlers by far, is Sesame Street. *It's fun, educational and entertaining for both my toddler and me."*

–HANNAH CHOW, M.D.

"Two equally favorite TV shows are Sesame Street *and* Blue's Clues. Sesame Street *has been a favorite since an early age – my son has always loved the colorful puppets, and I love the educational aspect (plus I find it very funny). My son learned a lot of letters and numbers from this show. Once he hit around two,* Blues Clues *joined the top of the list, and again, I think he's learned a lot from it. There are good messages, fun characters and story lines, and he tends to watch the shows on video again and again and memorizes the scripts."*

–SHARON LICHTENFELD

*"*Sesame Street, *without a doubt, is my favorite. It's educational and fun, and engages children in learning."*

–KAREN WILSON

*"*Blue's Clues *and* Dora the Explorer *are two of my kids' favorites. I like the way both shows encourage the kids to remember three clues to solve the puzzle or the three landmarks they must pass to get where they are going."*

–DANIELLE MARION-DOYLE

*"*Sesame Street *is by far, my favorite TV show. There is so much to learn from it, but it's fun. The characters are like old friends, and the*

songs are so memorable. It's timeless. I enjoyed watching it, and now my children do."

–KATE STEIMAN

"I like Dora, Oswald and Blue's Clues. My daughter, who is 2-1/2, gets so involved in these, especially playing along with Dora and Blue's Clues."

–ELICIA MOORE

"Blue's Clues is educational and entertaining. I think it teaches children excellent problem-solving skills."

–KRISTEN MATH

THE THREE BEST VIDEOS FOR BABIES AND TODDLERS

1. The Baby Einstein series – *Baby Mozart, Baby Shakespeare, Baby Van Gogh, Baby Doolittle,* etc.
2. Veggie Tales
3. The Wiggles

WHY WE LOVE THEM

"My favorite videos are the series by Baby Einstein. They show pictures of things that kids and babies love, like puppets and animals along with classical music and/or poetry. They are great for interacting with your child because you can point out colors or ask questions. That, and they are great to play when company is over: All you hear is classical music, and all you see are quiet, smiling children."

–CHELSEA COFFEY HAMMAN

"Baby Mozart *is the best video. I put Sam in his swing and in front of the TV to watch this at least three times a week so I can get dinner ready for my family. What a lifesaver!"*

–BETH MILLER

"My son Donovan (one year) loves all of the Baby Mozart *tapes. We have the entire collection, and he watches at least one tape a day. These are wonderful because they entertain your child for a full 30 minutes, and they are also learning at the same time. If it wasn't for these tapes, I would never be able to get the dishes done or take a shower! Donovan gets so excited when I put these videos in."*

–SARAH E. CAMPAGNA

"The Veggie Tales videos are wonderful for keeping toddlers and preschoolers interested, and they offer great moral lessons along with humor only adults would get."

–STEPHANIE HOSSZU

"I love The Wiggles. On rainy days, the girls really jump around to them, and I like the music. I resisted the urge to buy the tape for a long time, since they were the 'rage,' but I finally caved, and I am glad I did!"

–PATRICIA ARNOLD

"I like the Veggie Tales movies. Some people may be put off by the religious theme (though I'm not particularly religious, and I like them). They are fun stories with positive messages, catchy songs and no annoying dinosaurs!"

–KAREN WILSON

"The Baby Einstein videos are hands down the best for babies and toddlers. I particularly like the Baby Mozart *(classical music enhances learning),* Baby Doolittle *(teaches animals) and there are others that teach foreign language, etc."*

–BECKY GASTON

"I love all of The Wiggles videos. My toddler loves to dance along with all their catchy tunes."

–KATE STEIMAN

"My son adores Baby Mozart *and* Baby Bach. *It's 30 minutes where I can actually get something done because he's entranced by this video."*

–MICHELLE KOSEC

"We got a lot of use out of our collection of the Baby Einstein video series. He enjoyed watching them and learning from them. I liked them because they were simple enough for him to understand, but still taught him about shapes, colors, words and so on. I have friends that swear that Baby Einstein was the only way they got to take a shower when their children were infants."

–HEATHER FRENCH

CHAPTER 9:

Getting Organized Around the House

The word "multitasking" was probably invented by a mom. Sometimes it seems you need twelve arms to do everything you have to do in a day. That's why we've become experts at doing things quickly and efficiently. This chapter reveals our best tricks for organizing our homes, our time and our lives.

Saving Time in the Morning

The morning rush can be more stressful in your home than it is on a major highway, if you and/or the kid(s) have to go somewhere and you aren't organized. Here are the best ways to get everything done smoothly and efficiently.

OUR TOP TIPS FOR MAKING MORNINGS GO SMOOTHLY

1. Do as much as possible the night before.
2. Get ready before the kids get up.
3. Share the workload.
4. Shower at night.
5. Allow more time than you need to get ready.

HOW WE DO IT

"Make lunch the night before, get plenty of help from your husband, and most of all, get up really early so that mornings aren't rushed."

–LINDA LINGUVIC

"I make sure everyone's clothes are out the night before, right down to the socks and underwear, and I pack lunches and diaper bags the night before as well. That way, there is much less to do in the morning."

–BROOKE KUHNS

"I get my shower at night when my husband is home to make sure the kids are still asleep. I also like to pack the diaper bag and keep it, along with spare diapers, wipes and formula in the car."

–STEPHANIE R. SMITH

"I try to do as much as possible the night before – shower, lay out and iron clothes for work the next day, pack breakfast and lunch (which I eat at my desk in my private office), prepare the diaper bag for the sitter (extra diapers, clothes, etc.), have bottles of expressed breast milk packed in a little cooler in the fridge. I also put anything that can spend the night out into the car the night before. Since I nurse my daughter right before she goes to the sitter's, she arrives in her sleeper, and the sitter changes her into day clothes."

–CLAIRE BIENVENU

"As a full-time medical student and mother, I often have to do 'rounds' at the hospital by 6:30 a.m. One of the biggest morning time-saver tricks I do is to have everything ready the night before: diaper bag, clothes for myself and my son, showers/baths, breakfast plans, etc. This allows me to be up and out the door in 45 minutes. I also set the time on my alarm clock for 45 minutes ahead of the actual time. This way, I feel I am "sleeping in" and still can get to work on time."

–SYLVIA ANDERSON

"I often have to leave before my daughter wakes up in the morning, which leaves my husband to get our little girl ready. To make things easier on him (and me, so I don't have to see her in odd outfits), I put all of the parts of an outfit (socks included) into a big Ziploc bag as I'm folding and putting away laundry. That way, all he has to do is pick up a bag, and all the pieces are there."

–CHELSEA COFFEY HAMMAN

"I put my son's cereal in his bowl and cover it, so all I have to do is heat up his milk and pour it in the bowl in the morning. Also, I take my showers at night so I don't have to worry about it in the morning."

–ANNA MARIA JOHNSON

"The diaper bag is always packed and my husband's lunch is made the night before. I allow plenty of time, and I am proud to say I have still never been late for anything, even with twins."

–PATRICIA ARNOLD

"I usually prepare the night before. I purchase Lunchables™ or sometimes, I call the deli and let them know I'm on my way to drop my kids off to school. It is usually ready by the time I stop by."

–DAWN KIRNON, M.D.

"Always get up before your children! I try to get up early enough to have some quiet time, grab a cup of coffee, exercise, shower and dress before my children get up. Since my oldest is an early riser, I have to get started pretty early in order to accomplish this. On days when I am not able to, I find myself running two steps behind my children. I need that head start on the day and time to collect myself. Once I'm on track, I'm better able to tend to the needs of my children and oversee the things they are doing. It also leaves me more quality time to spend with them. It makes for an all-around better day."

–ANGELA SNODGRASS

"I usually shower in the evenings after my son has gone to bed. It saves time because it's usually my son who wakes me in the morning before the alarm does. I also bought a formula dispenser at Wal-Mart, and that helps out tremendously in the mornings. Instead of fumbling around with the can of formula and spilling it everywhere because I'm still half asleep, I just have the formula pre-measured in the dispenser and the water pre-measured in the bottle, so when I wake up, I just have to put the two together and shake it up."

–K. SCARLETT SHAW

"I take a shower at night and always plan what I am going to wear before I get out of bed. If I stand in front of the closet, it takes too long. I also always watch the weather to be sure to dress appropriately."

–SHELLY SOLOMON HUGGINS

THE SEVEN MOST-VALUABLE TOOLS FOR A TIME-CRUNCHED MOM

1. Online bill payment
2. Online shopping
3. A Palm® Pilot
4. Someone to clean the house
5. Online grocery shopping
6. Catalog shopping
7. Quicken®

WHY WE LOVE THEM

"I do online bill payment a lot. It saves money on stamps and is good for paying bills at the last minute."

–KEL BRIGHT

"Online bill payment is the best. Saves a ton of time – no checks to write, and I can transfer money from one account to the other in seconds."

–TAMARA PRINCE

"I do as much as possible online, especially anything financial, like banking and paying bills. I also shop online quite a bit. I love Quicken for keeping track of our finances, and I download all our banking and investment information every week."

–JAMIE HUNLEY

"I pay all my bills online through my bank, and it has been a tremendous time-saver. I also use automatic withdrawals as much as possible. I used to waste a lot of time shuffling papers and writing checks. Now all I have to do is just note the payment in my checkbook. No more trips to the post office."

–MICHELLE LANEY

"We pay all of our bills online or through automatic drafting. I hired a housekeeper to come in and clean twice a week. She is a lifesaver. And I write everything down in my day planner, since it goes everywhere with me."

–DEBORAH THERIAULT

"I've always used my Palm Pilot (long before mommying). It syncs with my PC, which I stare at all day. It beeps at me and fits in my purse. We pay some bills online, but grocery shopping, we do in person. Becca likes the store, so we go together."

–JENNIFER ROSE

"I couldn't survive without my Palm and my online calendar and reminders. I used to remember everything, but with three children and a large house to keep track of, I find I need a schedule. We pay all of our bills automatically with a credit card or online.

"My favorite time-saver is my cleaner! She keeps the mess down to a dull roar. I find that many husbands think that moms have lots of time to mother, feed, shop, do laundry, etc. and still clean. Very few of us do, and something has to go. In my case, it was my sanity until I hired Gloria."

–KATE HALLBERG

"I buy a lot of things through catalogs — easy things like sheets, toys and gifts for others. This saves so much time because just packing up the baby and his supplies for a shopping trip takes forever!"

—CARA VINCENS

"I absolutely love my Palm Pilot. I can't imagine what I would do without it. I keep a laptop computer in the kitchen and each morning, I pull up the daily schedule. All of the activities we are involved in are logged on to the Palm Pilot. I also keep my grocery list, miscellaneous shopping list, etc. on it. When I run out of something in the kitchen, I immediately log it onto the computer, and it gets logged onto the Palm Pilot at the next 'HotSync.' This has been an invaluable organizing tool. Wherever I am, I have our complete schedule, shopping lists, children's medication allergies, birthdays, etc. If I'm at the doctor's office, I can schedule a follow-up visit. If I'm out shopping, I always have a list of things I need with me."

—JULIE BARTLETT

"We use Quicken to manage our money and use online bill paying, which is a great time-saver. I use a master grocery shopping list that I post on the fridge, so that I don't have to make a new list every week. I also plan my meals weekly so grocery shopping is a breeze."

—HEATHER MEININGER

"I use Peapod (www.peapod.com; online grocery shopping service) at least once or twice a month, so I don't have to shop with two children in the cart. Saves me hours. We also go to Price Club to stock up on paper goods and other items. It cuts down on what you need at the grocery store and saves money, too. I cook in bulk (cook three meat loaves for dinner, eat one and freeze the other two). I use a Franklin Planner because I can jot notes/appointments quickly as needed and keep the family calendar."

—JENNIFER YOUNG

"Online gift shopping saves me the most time. CDs and books are so easy to find and send online."

—CAREN SADIKMAN, M.D.

SO WHAT DO YOU DO WITH ALL THAT STUFF?

Remember when it took less than ten minutes to clean up the clutter around your house in the evening? Then you had kids. And the older they get, the more they accumulate. When it comes to finding a place to store it all, we look for options that let us stow it when we don't want to use it, but allow us to easily find it when we do.

OUR NUMBER ONE CHOICE FOR STORING KIDS' TOYS AND STUFF

Rubbermaid plastic storage containers

WHY WE LOVE THEM

"They are inexpensive (around $4 each), they stack well, and they seal!"

–K. SCARLETT SHAW

"Our children can see through the plastic, so they know exactly what is inside each bin. Also, the containers stack neatly. The kids can easily carry around the small containers, taking them off the shelf or floor to wherever they want to play."

–SUSAN TACHNA

"I buy a lot of Rubbermaid containers and totes. They are durable, come in a variety of colors, easy to clean and fairly inexpensive."

– BECKY GASTON

"We buy storage bins that are big, clear plastic, and they stack. All of Bryce's toys go into them, and then for entertainment, he climbs on them to see if they'll hold. They do! They only cost about $4 each, so we can get many. They seem much safer to me than the usual toy boxes. Plus, you can look inside without un-stacking or opening them."

–SHERYL MADDEN

"I have one the same size as my son's toy box and got it for a fraction of the price."

–VERONICA WILSON

CLEANING UP: GETTING STAINS
OUT OF BABY CLOTHES

There's nothing cuter than a 10-month-old covered from head to toe in spaghetti sauce. But once you've taken a picture and plopped the munchkin in the bath, you're still faced with the problem of getting the clothes clean.

We recommend treating the stain as soon as possible. Even if you don't plan on washing the item right away, you can pre-treat the stain. Also, never put clothes in the dryer if the stain hasn't come out. Once they are dried, the stain is set.

BEST STAIN-FIGHTING PRODUCT

OxiClean®

WHY WE LOVE IT

"I have found that OxiClean is the only thing that works. The toughest stains I have had are ones on her bibs that have set for a while. I soak them in OxiClean overnight (sometimes) and the garment comes out looking brand new. It does not bleach."

–BECKY GASTON

"OxiClean worked wonders on my kids' white button-down shirts. They had eaten spaghetti and had gotten it all over the shirts along with some Kool-Aid®, and I just soaked them for about an hour-and-a-half, then threw them in the wash, and they came out great. I don't think even bleach would have taken those stains out."

–BROOKE ULINSKI

"OxiClean seems to get stains out of almost anything. My friend's daughters have a cream-colored carpet in their bedroom. It has had food, Kool-Aid, crayons, basically everything on it, and OxiClean has managed to get it all out and leave the carpet looking like new. It also worked on a crayon mishap in a dryer."

–KELLY HARDEN

"I have found that all of the children's stain lifters are basically all just a bunch of hype. I find that OxiClean works the very best, and if that won't take it out, nothing will!"

–REBECCA HARPER

"OxiClean works the best. I make a paste out of it and let it sit on the stain. The longer it sits, the better. I then wash the item in hot waster. The key is to make sure the stain is out before the item gets dried. Once it hits the dryer, the stain is set."

–MICHELLE LANEY

Displaying Kids' Artwork

Just as the plethora of baby gear begins to clear (the Exersaucer goes to a neighbor, the high chair gets put away, the crib gets stored downstairs), your kid hits preschool. Then you are deluged with artwork. Here's what to do with it.

OUR BEST IDEAS

"I like the idea of hanging a sort of clothesline in her room that we can hang her pictures on, using clothespins."

–CHAYA JAMIE REICH

"Decoupage it onto a wall or iron it onto a blanket. To iron on, first scan the artwork into your computer. Then get special iron-on transfer paper (sold at Wal-Mart or craft stores) and put that in your printer. Print out the artwork, and just iron on like any other transfers. You can make a carrying bag or T-shirts as well. They look really nice."

–VALERIE VICARS DOWNS

"One of the neatest ideas I have ever seen is to mount fairly large frames directly on the wall. You take a frame – no glass or backing – and hang it on the wall. You can then hang children's artwork on the wall (inside the frame) with the white tacky stuff that doesn't damage the walls. (It comes in little blocks; you can break off a piece and knead it, then stick things on the wall without any permanent damage to the wall.) Since it is not really framed, you can change artwork frequently, yet it really makes each piece look very special."

–SALLY FARRINGTON

"I put a plastic sheet on the play table — I believe you can get it at the Home Depot — and put their artwork underneath. Just put it on the table and tape it. After a few days/weeks, I ask my daughter if she wants to put something else under the sheet. If she says yes, we have fun choosing a new masterpiece and putting it under the plastic. Since her

daddy works away from the house all week, rotating the artwork has become a Friday ritual, a way to show daddy what she did that week."

–LAURENCE THELLIER

"I got a magnetic chalkboard from Pottery Barn. That way, my son can someday draw on the chalkboard, and we can use it to display his paper creations."

–BETH MILLER

"My daughter brings a new project home from preschool almost every day. At the end of each month, we hang all her artwork on our refrigerator and I take her picture standing next to it. That way, we can preserve the memories, but not have to store all of it."

–KIMBERLY MERCURIO, M.D.

"I really like the Pottery Barn Kids' frames that you can slide pictures in and out of."

–HEATHER FRENCH

Editor's note: These are called "Taylor Art Gallery Frames" in the Pottery Barn Kids Catalog

Saving Time in the Evening

They don't call it the "witching hour" for nothing. That one- to two-hour time span right before dinner is always crazy when you have little ones. You have to get dinner on the table. You have to clean up the clutter in the house and put away your own belongings from the car or work. You have to make sure they've done their homework and make sure you've done what you needed to do for the day. And you have to do it all before they melt down from exhaustion (or drive you insane!). Here are our best solutions for handling the evening rush.

OUR TOP TRICKS FOR TAKING THE EDGE OFF THE EVENING RUSH

1. Follow a routine.
2. Share the workload.
3. Cook in bulk, use the slow cooker and buy pre-made foods, such as cooked rotisserie chicken.

4. Start preparing dinner earlier in the day.

5. Skip the bath.

"A reasonable nighttime routine is essential for baby. We have a bath, breastfeed (even though he is on a schedule, he always eats right before bed regardless of the last time he ate), get PJs on with a nighttime diaper and rock while we sing the ABCs to him. Then it's into the bed after he's getting drowsy."

−KARI RYDELL

"My husband and I split the evening routine. One will give the girls their bath, while the other is cleaning the kitchen and picking up. That way, when the girls go to bed, everything is cleaned and we are not having to waste what little time we have alone picking up."

−MICHELLE LANEY

"I do as much dinner prep when my oldest is in school and my younger one is napping, as I can."

−SUSAN TACHNA

"I have found that Crock-Pot® cooking helps ease dinner pressures. It's easy to throw things in a Crock-Pot®, plug it in, and know that dinner will be ready when you get home."

−HANNAH CHOW, M.D.

"When making meat, I always cook enough for two-to-three meals. I cook enough chicken so we can eat chicken breasts one night, make stuffed chicken pasta shells the next and chicken wraps the third night."

−TAMARA PRINCE

"There's no law saying that kids need a bath each night. Unless there's a reason, we do a bath every other night."

−DONNICA L. MOORE, M.D.

"I have several things that work for me in the evenings. The first is minimizing effort with the evening meal by often cooking out of our freezer. This means defrosting a dish that I have previously made in quantity or preparing a frozen main dish item purchased from the store. I usually make rice or pasta to go with dinner and prepare some kind of vegetable (fresh or frozen).

−SIDNEY MARKS

"The hour before dinner tends to be very hectic — calming down from the day and coming in the house grubby from play takes up a good portion of dinner preparation time. What I do is prepare dinner in the middle of the day (when feasible). I enjoy this 'quiet' time of the day preparing our family meals. Lots of Crock-Pot ® meals, soups, egg noodle dishes, salads — things I only have to reheat just before sitting down to the meal.

"When I do it this way, the hour before mealtime is used for cleaning up the living area, organizing homework assignments, breaking up sibling arguments, etc., supervising children's chores, bringing laundry to the laundry room, etc. When we do sit down, the kids are clean, the house is tidy, the meal is prepared stress-free, and Daddy comes home to a loving, warm family dinner."

–LORI BURGESS

"Dinner is always a challenge. Friday evening is always pizza night. We usually eat fast food one other evening during the week (whenever we are busiest). I have a list of quick meals that I rotate. I also cook during the weekend, so there is at least one meal of leftovers."

–KAREN HAAS

"Some days if we're home early and the kids need a bath, I'll bathe them at 4 p.m. before dinner instead of waiting until after when everyone is starting to have a meltdown. I like to keep a few prepared dinners in the freezer for those nights when you don't have time to cook."

–KATE STEIMAN

"Prepare food in advance. When my kids were little, I used to do all my cooking on Sundays. I worked and wanted to just be able to heat something up fast."

–LINDA LINGUVIC

"My husband is 'the bath man.' While I clean up the kitchen after dinner, he gives our four and two-year-olds a bath. They really enjoy that time with him, and it allows me to have a few minutes of quiet."

–KIMBERLY MERCURIO, M.D.

"I cook a portion or all of my meal for the next night (sometimes this is not possible, but it sure saves time when I can). We have leftover night once a week, and this is the night that the refrigerator gets cleaned out. If we don't eat it, it gets tossed."

–DONNA DAVIDSON

I did hire a housekeeper to clean twice a month. This is the best money I've ever spent. It frees up my time, and I feel like my house is clean. Of course, I still have to pick up and do laundry, etc., but this has taken a load off of me."

–BRANDY CHARLES

In the Mood for a Quickie?
Try These Fast and Easy Recipes

The biggest challenge of the evening rush for most of us is getting dinner ready before the kids meltdown. Here are our favorite time-saving meals.

OUR FAVORITE QUICK-DINNER RECIPES

"Mix pasta with veggies, any jar sauce (usually sun-dried tomato) and a salad on the side."

K. SCARLETT SHAW

"Chop a half a zucchini, 1/2 cup of carrots and 1/2 cup of broccoli. Put it in a pot with 1/2 cup of orzo. Add enough water to cover. Bring to a boil and cook until the orzo is done. Drain, add a couple of tablespoons of butter (more if you would like), 1/2 cup of Parmesan cheese and a chopped cooked chicken breast. Yummy."

–PATRICIA ARNOLD

"I keep an assortment of pasta and canned, seasoned diced tomatoes on hand. In about 15 minutes, I can have a basic pasta dish on the table. With a few more minutes and the addition of some shredded cheese and/or some cottage cheese(cream cheese is good too), I can have a nice quick pasta casserole ready to serve."

–LYNN PARKS

"Broccoli and Pasta with Garlic — *Steam broccoli. Boil pasta (any kind will do). Chop garlic and saute in olive oil. When pasta and broccoli are done, throw them in frying pan with the olive oil and garlic. Stir, sprinkle with Parmesan cheese, and you are all set!"*

–REBECCA ALDER

"I take 1 pound of browned ground beef, 1 box of Velveeta Shells & Cheese (cooked per directions), 1/2 cup sour cream, salt, pepper, chili powder (optional). Combine all the ingredients for a creamy chili mac."

–KELI LOVELAND

"Ginger Chicken for Two — Dice two chicken breasts. Fry them lightly in oil. Meanwhile, slice one small onion and a small peeled ginger root. Take the chicken out of the pan. Set aside. Fry the vegetables on low heat for five minutes until soft. Add chicken, lemon juice to taste, season and serve with rice."

–LAURENCE THELLIER

"Chicken and gravy or beef tips and gravy over pasta."

KAREN HAAS

"I throw chicken breasts or thighs, a jar of salsa, a package of taco powder seasoning, 1/2 to 1 cup of water, a 15 ounce can of black beans and a 15 ounce can of kidney beans into the Crock-Pot® and cook all day long. When I get home, I use my rice cooker to make 1-1/2 cups cooked rice, which I throw into the Crock-Pot® after it's cooked. Then I top it with shredded Mexican cheese mix."

–MICHELE F. CARLON, M.D.

"You can mix together whatever is in the fridge and serve it over pasta with frozen veggies, and it seems like a good, home-cooked meal. Other than the traditional tomato-based sauces, I've used cooked chicken and broccoli with a little oil and garlic, ground beef and peppers, and just about any type of meat/fish/poultry with a cream of mushroom soup. You're limited only by your imagination and your kids' tastes.

–JULIA WONDERLING

"Fish sticks and tater tots!"

–LISA MCDONALD

"I'm a pseudo-vegetarian. This is my favorite: 1/2 cup coarsely chopped red onions, 1/2 cup coarsely chopped green peppers, 1/2 cup coarsely chopped mushrooms, 2 tablespoons olive oil, pepper and garlic to taste, 1 teaspoon parsley flakes, 1-1/2 cups cooked white rice. Preheat oven to 350. Place vegetables into a lasagna pan or other suitable metal pan. Stir in olive oil, pepper, garlic and parsley flakes. Bake for 20-25 minutes stirring, occasionally. Serve over cooked white rice; season to taste with soy sauce."

–KAREN HURST

"Broiled Salmon in Teriyaki Sauce with Pineapple — *Marinate the salmon in teriyaki sauce and broil 7-9 minutes on each side with pineapple. Goes great with rice and asparagus."*

–ELIZA LO CHIN, M.D.

"Our favorite quick dinner is a Crock-Pot® meal. Take an inexpensive cut of beef, such as a chuck roast, place in Crock-Pot® and top with a jar of your favorite salsa. Let cook on low all day. The meat easily shreds apart. Serve with warm tortillas, shredded cheese, lettuce and more salsa. Sometimes we add a can of two of beans to the Crock-Pot® midway through the day."

–SALLY FARRINGTON

"Pasta with spaghetti sauce and cottage cheese mixed in. Nice protein and calcium boost."

–SARAH PLETCHER

"Chicken and Rice — *Preheat oven to 375. In a 13 x 9 baking dish, melt 1 stick of butter. Pour over butter, 1-1/2 cups of raw long grain rice. Add salt and pepper to taste. Place about 5 boneless skinless chicken breasts on top of the rice. Sprinkle one package of Lipton's Onion Soup Mix over everything. Pour 3 cups of water over this. Cover tightly with foil and bake 1-1/2 hours. You can double the recipe and put one pan in the freezer for a later date. It's great reheated also."*

–TRACI BRAGG, M.D.

"Rebecca's One Dish Pasta Casserole — *1 bag of pasta (any kind will do; I like rotini), 1 pound of ground meat, your choice (beef, chicken, etc.), 1 large jar of tomato sauce or 1 medium-small jar of sauce and 1 can of tomatoes, 1 onion, chopped mushrooms (canned or fresh; canned is fastest; if fresh, then chopped), frozen veggies (corn is our family favorite), grated cheese.*

Fry ground meat and onions while boiling water. Add mushrooms to fry pan in the last few minutes. (I have found that boiling the water in the kettle is a lot faster than waiting for it to boil in the pot if you are in a big hurry.) When water has boiled, add pasta and frozen veggies. Cook until pasta is done. Strain. In pot or CorningWare dish, mix pasta mixture, cooked meat mixture and tomato products. Stir well. Sprinkle cheese over top. Place in a preheated 350 oven until cheese is melted and sauce is warm."

–REBECCA CURTIS

When You Can't Face Going Into the Kitchen

Sure, these recipes are great, but sometimes you just don't have the time or energy to cook another meal. When that's the case, here's where to go.

OUR THREE FAVORITE PLACES FOR FAST FOOD

1. McDonald's®
2. Wendy's®
3. Chick-fil-A®

WHY WE RECOMMEND THEM

"McDonald's is our favorite place to go. It has the playground for our three-year-old."

–BARBARA EVANS

"My girls love Wendy's. It's one of our favorite fast food spots."

–DAWN KIRNON, M.D.

"I like Chick-fil-A. I can get healthier food there, and the kid's meal toys are normally books or books on tape. It's a nice change from all the tie-in toys that end up as junk soon anyway."

–BRENDA BROWN

"McDonald's is not the healthiest place on the planet, but you can't beat a Happy Meal® to cheer up cranky kids."

–BROOKE KUHNS

"I like McDonald's because it is the closest to my house, they have a fairly decent drive-through, and the under-three-year-old toys are pretty decent."

–DONNA DAVIDSON

"For taste, I prefer Chick-fil-A, but we don't have it in our area. In our area, Wendy's is the healthiest in my opinion."

–DONNICA L. MOORE, M.D.

"Chick-fil-A has good, fresh food that is not overloaded with 'stuff.' They have a nice small playground that is always clean and never packed like the McDonald's playground. The restaurant itself is always clean. Overall, a great place to eat."

–DANA A. CROY

"I like Wendy's for a fast food dinner. I find they have the most options for me to still eat healthy while getting a quick food fix. The chili (without cheese) and a baked potato (without butter or sour cream) are filling and low in fat."

–LISA BITTAR

"I would have to say Chick-fil-A! Their chicken nuggets are whole chicken pieces, and their fries are great. Also, they are a Christian-based company and are not opened on Sunday, so that employees can spend time with their families. They are also a good place for a teenager to work. They are good with them and give scholarships for college."

–TRISH HALE

"Wendy's is fast and good, and they have the best chicken nuggets ever!"

–NINA MCCANN

"I like McDonald's. The food is quick, they have lots of choices – hamburger, chicken, even pizza at some places, enough choices to make any child happy. And they are very friendly."

–VALERIE VICARS DOWNS

"I like Wendy's because you can get baked potatoes, salads, etc. that you can't get at the other restaurants. Plus, there is no Chick-fil-A or Arby's® anywhere near us."

–TRACY PRITCHARD

"Chick-fil-A has good food, reasonably-priced and it's Christian-owned."

–SHELLY SOLOMON HUGGINS

"We usually go to McDonald's because of the play area, but I prefer the food at Wendy's."

–PATRICIA ARNOLD

"I would have to say I like Wendy's because their food is better quality, and the kids get a dessert with their meal."

–ELICIA MOORE

"I love the chili at Wendy's."

–DEBORAH THERIAULT

CHAPTER 10:

Family Fun and Rituals

You don't exactly take a baby or toddler to an amusement park for fun, but there are things you can do together that are enjoyable for both of you. Here are our favorites.

Our Nine Favorite Outings With Little Ones

1. Park or playground
2. Take a walk
3. Beach
4. Zoo
5. Picnic
6. Hiking
7. Swimming
8. Feed the ducks
9. Visit the grandparents

WHY WE LOVE THEM

"My daughter and I go to the park early in the morning. She sits on my shoulders while I walk fast around the lake. I point out all of the animals and the sounds they make for my daughter...and I get an extra workout with the 20+ pounds on my shoulders!"

–GENEVIEVE MOLLOY

"My favorite activity with my daughter, 14-months, is going to the park. There is a fantastic tot lot there, and she really lights up on the swings! When she laughs and squeals like that, nothing else compares!"

–MEGAN MARTIN

"I take him to the swimming pool or any other water-related activity. I like it because I myself love water and want him to love it, too. He loves it because he gets to watch a lot of other kids play."

–KRISZTINA RAB

"With only a 5-month-old, our favorite outing is visiting either set of grandparents. Both of our son's grandfathers love taking Noah outside. He will stay outside (in the shade, of course) with both of them for one to two hours."

–DANA A. CROY

"My favorite regular outing with her would have to be our walks at the beach. We go after dinner, and she loves sitting in her carriage and seeing all the babies in their carriages and all the dogs on their leashes."

–DONNA DAVIDSON

"We love to just take walks around the block. It gives us bonding time while keeping everyone relaxed and sometimes putting the kids to sleep."

–JESSICA GANE

"I love to go with Kirstin for a walk. We walk hand in hand and enjoy the trees, the grass and every living thing we come into contact with. A simple walk with her is delightful, especially in the morning when the birds are still chirping quietly. My daughter is just now beginning to parrot my speech, so we can spend endless time pointing out things that are new to her vocabulary."

–SHELLY SOLOMON HUGGINS

"This summer, we created a 'drive-in' in our driveway. The boys take turns selecting a movie, and we open the windows in the van and watch the movie on the van TV. I make popcorn, and the boys each get a soda before we head outside. They love the fact that they can talk at our movie, and it is an inexpensive way to give them a special night. (Our neighbors think we are a little strange when they catch us sitting in our van that long.)"

–LORI STUSSIE

How We Make Them Feel Special

We all want to make our kids feel loved. Here's our best advice for showing love to little ones in the early years.

TIPS FROM THE TRENCHES

✓ **Laugh, dance and sing together.**

"Every morning when Dylan wakes up, I lean over the crib, smile at him and say, 'I spy with my little eye my cute l'il pumpkin pie, and he cuts up laughing. It starts his day out with a smile and mine, too. We also dance together. He likes it and I think the closeness is good for him, too."

—KELLY HARDEN

✓ Celebrate for no reason.

"A great, little thing that makes kids happy is to celebrate just because! Make and decorate a cake together and celebrate any little accomplishment or just the fact that it's Tuesday."

—CARA VINCENS

✓ Write letters or keep a journal.

"When I found out I was pregnant with each of my boys, I bought a blank book. I write in each of them as often as possible and record the little milestones or funny things they say. I include pictures occasionally, and I tell each one why they are so special or unique. When they are older, I will give them their books, so they will have a history of my love affair with them."

—LORI STUSSIE

✓ Make up a special song.

"They each have their own little songs that my mom made up for them. My oldest even sings his to himself, and my younger son is starting to sing his, too. I think that it makes them feel very special to have their own little songs that we sing to them when they are getting ready to go to sleep."

—BROOKE ULINSKI

✓ Make getting up fun.

"When my daughter goes to bed, I sneak around hiding her toys. I put some in her refrigerator, in the plastic eggs left over from Easter, in her block box...anything I can hide things in. She LOVES to wake up and find her toys in new places. Then she comes over and throws herself in my arms!"

—GENEVIEVE MOLLOY

✓ Spend time one on one.

"The biggest thing is to try to get time alone with each of them. We have started instituting 'mommy' and 'daddy' days when each of us takes one with us for a special time. Home Depot can be very exciting when it is special time with daddy."

–PATRICIA ARNOLD

Birthday Parties

There is only one hard and fast rule about planning kids' birthday parties: They should be designed so the birthday kid has fun (while this may seem like an obvious concept, it doesn't always work out that way).

EIGHT GREAT SECRETS FOR BIRTHDAY PARTY SUCCESS

1. Make sure it is age-appropriate.
2. Make it easy on yourself.
3. Limit the number of guests.
4. Do it at home.
5. Keep it simple.
6. Give it a theme.
7. Have a game plan.
8. Do it outside.

"When my children (now in their thirties) were growing up, we just had our friends and their children over to the house, put up balloons and served coffee, birthday cake and ice cream. Basically, I think it's the people who make the party, not the fancy place where everyone tries to outdo each other."

–LINDA LINGUVIC

"When she turned 1, I didn't want to go all out because I knew she would get overstimulated and wouldn't remember it anyway. We had a small Winnie the Pooh party with close relatives. I have to say it was the best party I have ever seen. Turned out great."

–BECKY GASTON

"I have learned that I do not have to go all out or compete with my children's friends when planning parties. Just as long as the focus is on my birthday child, we all have a good day."

–KELI LOVELAND

"The best party I have thrown was a bowling party. It was not a lot of money. They set up, played games with the kids, gave us our own room for lunch, cake and gifts, and they cleaned up!"

–ELICIA MOORE

"That rule you always hear (and that I always ignored) about the number of guests being the kid's age plus one should be a mantra for all mothers!"

–DONNICA L. MOORE, M.D.

"Try to think like the children you are planning for. For instance, what would cause an argument among 5-year-olds...'Johnny got a blue whistle, and I got a red one. I want a blue one!' If you think like they do, you can avoid tears and help everyone have fun, including the adults."

–COLLEEN GRACE WEAVER

"The home parties with planned activities – treasure hunt in the backyard, piñata, games, etc. can be just as fun as the ones at a special party place – and much less expensive. You can even put more money into the party favors and still end up ahead."

–ELIZA LO CHIN, M.D.

"Though there is less clean-up work if you have the party somewhere else, the best parties are definitely at home where your child can show their friends their room and play together. If the other parents stay, this also gives you the opportunity to get to know each other."

–KRISTEN MATH

"I always keep the parties simple for my boys. They get to pick the theme and invite a few friends and family. Cake, ice cream, presents and free play for the kids in my home."

–WENDY DOUGLAS

"We had a monster birthday party. We had a 'monster stomp' activity where the kids stomped on balloons (monsters), 'Pin the Eye on the Monster' (Mike from Monsters, Inc.) and made monster puppets for the

craft. The theme was orange and green, so we had orange and green balloons, streamers, napkins and plates. I served orange and green Kool-Aid and had all snacks in orange and green cups."

–DENINE SCALLEN

"This year, we are throwing a wizard party, where the kids will make wizard hats, have wands, do an obstacle course and a treasure hunt."

–KAREN SULTAN

"I am a preschool teacher and have helped lots of moms plan parties. Young children need some planned activities or they go crazy. Having a game plan for the party is a great idea. I once helped plan a Halloween birthday party. I made a timetable list for the mother to use. We planned the two hours so that every 10 to 15 minutes, there was something new to do. From arriving, eating and activities, the two hours flew by and there was no chaos. The kids had a great time, and the parents that stayed enjoyed it as well."

–SUSAN DOBRATZ

"I would say the best was one that was at a picnic area on the outside of a playground. It was really nice for the kids to be able to go and play, then come back to the picnic area and eat after a cookout."

–VERONICA WILSON

CHAPTER 11:

Answers to Your Most Frequently Asked Questions

1. How can I get my baby to sleep?

"I have always found that you're better off to let the baby learn to put themselves to sleep. As soon as they look/act tired, lay them down, give a kiss and go. They really do get into habits, and this one is very important. I really feel that you should avoid using a pacifier at night time, but if that is the only way your baby is soothed, take the pacifier out of their mouths as soon as they are asleep. This way, you don't have to keep getting up to get it if it falls out, and they won't wake up looking for it all the time."

−STACI PARO

"Try to keep a daily routine with naps and bedtime. My baby learned it was wake, eat, play, sleep and repeat, with a bath before bed as well. I was able to set her down and she would go to sleep on her own most times."

−TAMARA PRINCE

"I think it is essential to stick with the same bedtime routine each night. For the last feeding, we keep it very low key − minimum lighting, whispering, etc. He conks out during that last feeding, even to the point where he is just about asleep. He is then put into his crib where he just falls asleep. Even though he doesn't always go to sleep at the same time every night, his routine is always the same."

−APRIL MCCONNELL

"Rocking, walking the baby, darkening the room so the baby knows it's time to sleep."

−SHANNON GUAY

"At 6 weeks, we started putting her to sleep in her crib. I used to give her a bottle first, but then it got to be harder and harder. Finally, we just decided to put her down awake and walk away. After three nights, she

was sleeping through the night with no problems. I never read the Ferber book [Solve Your Child's Sleep Problems by Richard Ferber], but it is the Ferber method. To make it easier, I recruited some mom friends who were willing to try it at the same time. We would call each other to talk, and that made it easy for the crying nights in the beginning."

–SUSAN DOBRATZ

"Johnson's® lavender baby soap, a full bottle and a lullaby. Works like a charm."

–BROOKE KUHNS

2. What is the best way to soothe a colicky baby?

"Wrap them in a blanket really tight and hold them."

–CRYSTAL SHOULTS

"What worked for me was to put the baby in the swing or run the vacuum cleaner. Sometimes I had to do both at once."

–BECKY GASTON

"The shower, the shower, the shower!!! When my son had colic, we discovered that the sound of a running shower stopped his crying instantly. My husband and I would take turns sitting in the bathroom while he listened to the shower...ahhh, the good old days!"

–STACI PARO

"A lot of pacing around and swaying with them in your arms helps. Try different 'white noises,' such as a clothes dryer, hair dryer, etc. Friends of ours had a bad time with their first daughter with colic, and the only way they could all sleep at night was to leave a hair dryer running all night long in their bathroom."

–REBECCA HARPER

"I found that laying her across my knees belly down and gently rocking back and forth helped. Also, giving her a full-body baby massage really helped. I gently rub her back, legs, arms and belly, as if I were putting on lotion; I just rub a little longer. Some hospitals offer classes in infant massage. Also, a web site I found helpful was www.infantmassage.com."

–BOBBI ANNAL

"We found when our first son had colic, that a swing was indispensable. We moved it from room to room through the day so he could always see

me. When the swinging wasn't enough, we made a sort of tea from a few fennel seeds boiled in a few ounces of water until it was black, with a pinch of sugar. Three ounces of this in a small bottle settled the colic better than any commercial gas drops we tried, and the pediatrician approved it as safe."

–DEBBIE PALMER

"Remove all dairy from mom's diet if she is breastfeeding. Dairy intolerance is common and painful. Buy a sling (Maya Wrap is a great brand) and use it to wear the baby when she is fussy. Most importantly, remember that babies don't stay colicky forever, and this too shall pass."

–MEGAN MILES

"Go for long rides in the car. But also, don't be afraid to ask your pediatrician about it to see if your baby has reflux. Many so-called colicky babies actually have acid reflux, and it causes them great pain."

–AMELIA STINSON-WESLEY

"It depends on the source of the colic. Get a good family health book to troubleshoot possible physical causes of unhappiness (teething, hunger, tired, constipation, gas, etc.). A lot of babies have a 'witching hour' in the early evening/afternoon when the crying is at its worst. I found that taking my son outside helped a great deal. Being outdoors kept him diverted very nicely. You can also try various measures to address possible bowel discomfort – bicycling their legs, putting them tummy down on a firm surface (your lap, forearm, etc.), burping, over-the-counter gas medicine, etc.

"Lastly, the most important thing is to correctly frame your role in the crying. Sometimes if you take the attitude that you are not supposed to try to end the crying, but rather, be supportive during the crying, it will ease YOUR tension, which helps to settle the baby. Remember, it is hard to be a baby! Think of all the organs that are growing so quickly, the GI system is developing at such a fast rate, etc. They are learning to eat and digest and breathe outside the womb. Not to mention the fact that they are adjusting to all the stimulation thrown at them for the first time. If you are empathetic and supportive of them when they are having growing pains, things will get better."

–SARAH PLETCHER

"Running the vacuum works wonders, as does running water or the shower in the bathroom. You'll get hot while in there, but it worked for *my daughter…or maybe the steam just wore her out."*

–TAMARA PRINCE

"It's important to distinguish between the normal 'fussy period' that babies have, versus true colic, which is fussiness and discomfort, which seems to happen for more than two hours a day on a daily basis and where other medical causes have been ruled out. Through the years, many different remedies have been tried. First off, if you are breastfeeding, try to see if something in your diet may be making the baby irritable. Common culprits are milk, caffeine, spicy foods and certain vegetables, such as cabbage. If you are bottle-feeding, a change in formula type – from milk-based to soy-based, for example – will sometimes alleviate the symptoms.

Taking the legs and drawing them up into the knee-chest position and then bicycling them has also helped babies to pass gas if that is the cause of the colicky symptoms. Other remedies which have helped some babies include simethicone drops (Mylicon or Gerber gas drops), Hyland's Colic Tablets or chamomile tea. If using the tea, remember that baby needs milk as the main source of nutrition, and tea does not have the calories or electrolytes that the baby needs. So if you are giving the tea, it is recommended to give it not more than once or twice a day, and only one to two ounces per feeding.

"Some babies, despite all the above or other remedies tried, will continue to have colic. It can be a very trying and stressful time for parents, but try to remember that colic is not forever. It will probably go away by the time the baby is around 4 months old if not sooner."

–DIANE BEDROSIAN, M.D.

3. How can I relieve soreness from nursing?

"I experienced lots of discomfort. I definitely recommend cabbage leaves (on your breasts) but only for ten minutes or it will dry up your milk. Make sure they are very cold. Also, massaging them while in the shower to express some milk works."

–ANNA MARIA JOHNSON

"Frozen peas are your best friend. Trust me."

–BROOKE KUHNS

"I found that warm showers helped tremendously, as did making sure that I pumped once the pain started. Pumping can do wonders for breast pain. I also had some nipple discomfort and rawness the first couple of

weeks. The Medela breast cream is wonderful and really softened my nipples and the skin around it."

–DANA A. CROY

"For cracked nipples, I would always rub breast milk on my nipples when she finished nursing. I would let them air dry. Also, the greatest thing I found to help this was using Bag Balm (www.bagbalm.com). It is actually a cream used for cows' teats.

"I first found out about Bag Balm through a friend who recommended it. I checked around the Internet a bit and found some postings on various parenting web sites where people were using it for cracked nipples as well as diaper rashes. They said it was recommended by their doctors and pediatricians. I asked a midwife about it, and she said it was great. Although not recommended for children, she said she knew many people who used it and got great relief from it. It is a thicker ointment that tends to give nice coverage between nursing. The main ingredient is lanolin, but it is much thicker and lasts longer than other creams I tried.

"I have heard some people say to wash nipples well before nursing, but others said they have not bothered. I would quickly wash with soap and water first."

–TAMARA PRINCE

"What I discovered helped the most was to pump a little bit before putting the babies on my breast. I found that my breasts were so full that the babies were latching on to my nipples instead of the areola. If I pumped first, my breasts were soft enough for them to latch on properly."

–SHERRY RENNIE

"Sore nipples are quite common when nursing is first getting established. It can be very painful and the nipples can sometimes bleed. Expressed breast milk, massaged into the nipple area, will help with this.

Another new innovation which has been a lifesaver for many are glycerin pads that are available at Babies "R" Us and also from most lactation consultants. These pads are placed in your bra after nursing. They feel cold and are so very soothing!"

–DIANE BEDROSIAN, M.D.

"I did use the Lansinoh® ointment after each feeding because right at the beginning – still in the hospital – I had a little bit of cracking and bleeding. The ointment works great. I also experienced engorgement when my milk initially came in and as she slept longer stretches and through the night. Easy enough to remedy by pumping to comfort. The best advice I got in relation to nursing was to give it 40 days. At that point, baby knows what she is doing, your breasts and nipples have adjusted, and you feel confident. Nursing is now pain-free, and I feel like I really connect with my daughter, especially after a long day at work."

–CLAIRE BIENVENU

"I had cracked nipples in the hospital when my third child was two days old. He had a barracuda-like latch. My other children did not have such strong sucks, so that was new to me. The water from the shower felt like fire on my nipples. My lactation consultant recommended breast shields so my clothes wouldn't touch the cracked areas, and also recommended slathering on Lansinoh cream after each feeding. It was painful, but got much better after a week, so I no longer had to wear the shields."

–KIMBERLY MERCURIO, M.D.

"Take a disposable diaper soaked in hot water, then apply it to the breast for engorgement. For nipples, try the special bandages to be applied on burns. This cools the nipples and helps them heal when they are raw and bleeding."

–DENINE SCALLEN

"For clogged ducts, soak your breast in a bowl of water as hot as you can stand (or take a hot bath) twice a day, and nurse, nurse, nurse."

–AMELIA STINSON-WESLEY

"The biggest thing is to make sure baby is latched on properly. If you let her get used to latching on the wrong way, she won't get milk as easily and your nipples will hurt like heck!"

–JULIE WONDERLING

"Nursing should not be uncomfortable. If it is, it is important to find out the reason and solve the problem quickly. The most common cause of discomfort is the baby latching on incorrectly. If this is the case, contact a qualified lactation consultant who can guide you through the latching on process (you can call Medela's breastfeeding hotline at 1-800-TELL-YOU for more information). Another common cause of discomfort is cracked or dry nipples. These can be avoided and treated by expressing a small amount of milk at the end of each nursing session and rubbing it into the nipple, then allowing the nipple to air dry. Severe cases can be treated with lanolin products such as Lansinoh, which help seal in the moisture.

"A third and important cause to rule out is yeast infection. One way to check this is to look in the baby's mouth for thrush — white patches on the tongue and cheeks. If these are present speak to your pediatrician. Yeast infections need to be treated simultaneously in the mother and baby or they will continue to pass back and forth between the two. They may be treated with nystatin (liquid for baby, cream for you) and should be treated until all symptoms are gone and then for three-to-four more days to ensure that the organism is completely gone. At the same time, anything that goes in the baby's mouth (like a pacifier or nipple from a bottle) should be sterilized at least once a day, and bras should be changed frequently and washed in hot water."

–RIVKA STEIN, M.D.

4. Do you have any tips or tricks for trimming a squirming baby's fingernails?

"Trim fingernails while baby is sleeping, if at all possible. If baby is awake, hold his hand so all of his fingers show, and snip all five nails quickly, then take a cuddle break before doing the other hand."

–DEBBIE PALMER

"I usually do it before bedtime while he's in my lap watching Barney and being mellow."

–LISA MCDONALD

"When Liam was little we were firm believers in cutting them while he was asleep. Now that he is almost two, we cut them while he watches in amazement. He thinks it's fascinating."

–HEATHER FRENCH

"As silly as this sounds, I was much more comfortable biting my newborns' fingernails. They are just so little, and I was so afraid of cutting them with scissors or clippers, so I would feel with my tongue and teeth and was able to keep them very well groomed that way until they got big enough that I could hold their little fingers still enough to trim with scissors or clippers."

–SHERRY RENNIE

5. What is the best way to wean a baby off of the bottle?

"Start them sucking on a sippy cup at around 5 months to get the hang of what it is. Then when you think it is time to take it away, just give

them the cup. Take turns throughout the day switching back and forth between cup and bottle, and they will get used to the cup and eventually won't want the bottle."

–CRYSTAL SHOULTS

"I used the Avent® bottles, which have an insert that turns them into a sippy cup, so it was not so unfamiliar when we made the switch. It was then an easy switch to regular sippy cups."

–JULIE BARTLETT

"We first took away the daytime bottles, and she had a bottle just at night and in the morning. Then we took away the morning bottle for a month or two, and then we took the nighttime bottle away. We just felt that taking it away all at once would be too traumatic for her."

–DONNA DAVIDSON

"I would offer the sippy cup continuously until it "clicked" for my daughter. Just don't quit trying!"

–ERIKA PLODZIEN

"If they are eating food they really like, they will give up the daytime bottle. And at night, set up a routine that does not include the bottle right before they go to sleep."

–SABRINA LANE

"How about waiting until the baby is ready to give it up? Our pediatrician told me I had to wean our baby at age 1. My older son's pediatrician said I had to wean him at age 2. Where do they come up with these magic numbers? With my older son, I didn't know better, so I followed the doctor's recommendation and had him weaned at 2 with quite a struggle. He was not interested in any new cups, designer cups, etc. He would cry for his bottle, but I stood firm. It took a good week before he adjusted and accepted.

"This time around, I told the pediatrician NO. All the babies I am acquainted with who were weaned at age one are still sucking on pacifiers, even at age 3. Little Bryce, my 2-1/2 -year-old, gave up his bottle yesterday with no replacements required. He has not once asked for his bottle, and is quite capable now of taking a nap or going down for the night without one.

"This somewhat new idea of turning our little ones into little adults drives me crazy! There is way too much input from others as to what ages our children should be doing certain things. If we would pay closer attention to our children, rather than the so-called experts, I believe we would have happier kids, happier parents and a whole lot less stress in our daily lives."

–SHERYL MADDEN

6. What is the best way to get rid of a pacifier?

"Two words: Cold turkey. We picked a weekend and just stopped giving it to her."

–DONNA DAVIDSON

"I cut a hole in my daughter's pacifier and when she put it in her mouth, she spit it out. We had a rough couple of nights, but all is well."

–ELICIA MOORE

"My doctor told me at my son's six-month check-up that I should start to only give him the pacifier at night and not as something to occupy him. My husband and I left the office without the pacifier in our son's mouth and from that day on, he never craved it. A few nights later, I couldn't get him to relax to burp before bed, so I grabbed the pacifier and placed it in his mouth and he spit it out. I thought that it popped out in his struggles for comfort and replaced it in his mouth, and again, out it popped. I couldn't believe it. Even when my son saw other children with pacifiers in their mouths, he didn't mind at all."

–ANITA GOOD

"I have read several wonderful ways to help them let go of them, however my son is not old enough to use these tactics yet. I read in a magazine about a father that got his daughter to plant hers in the backyard, and that night, he planted a beautiful blooming bush in the hole, so the next morning, she had her 'paci plant.' I have also heard of the paci fairy that comes at night and takes the pacis to babies who need them and leaves gifts for the child who has outgrown them."

–HEATHER FRENCH

"We gave away all pacifiers to the Easter Bunny. We told my son that once the last one was lost or broken, there would be no more. After two weeks, I snipped off the very tip of the pacifier, and he didn't want it because it was broken. We had one hard night, but he was pacifier free from that point on."

–DENINE SCALLEN

"With our second child, we were so busy that we started using a pacifier that she called her 'nutti.' Weaning her proved to be quite challenging, so we decided one day that the 'nutti fairy' wold come and take away her pacifier and leave her a gift in its place. I rounded up all the pacifiers ahead of time so that she just had one. She placed it under her pillow and the next morning, there was a dolly in its place. That was the end of the nuttis. With baby number three, we decided that prevention was the best cure. We breastfed on demand and left the pacifiers in the store."

–KRISTEN MATH

7. How can I get my toddler to transition to a big bed from the crib?

"Involve your child in the process. Talk about how much she has grown and mention the things she can do now that she could not do when she was a baby. Use this as a base for introducing the idea of moving to a new bed. Let your child move their favorite blanket or stuffed animal and help you set up the new bed."

–ELICIA MOORE

"My kids are close in age. My oldest son was 18 months old when he gave up his crib to let his baby brother sleep in the crib. It was him doing it on his own. He was thrilled to sleep in his bed with Mickey Mouse sheets and blankets."

–CONNIE CHOATE

"Let them be a part of the process – picking out the bed, moving their toys to the bed, making the bed, etc."

–SABRINA LANE

"I put the bed in his room for a week or so before I actually had him sleep in it at all. Then we started with just naps. After that, he actually asked to sleep in it and said the crib was 'for babies.'"

–BROOKE KUHNS

"We bought her a little toddler bed and made a big fuss about her 'princess bed' and she couldn't wait to sleep in it."

–KATE STEIMAN

"We waited until he was receptive. We would visit the bed departments at stores and think about it, but I waited until he wanted a big bed. Generally, waiting until a child initiates a major change (whenever possible) or at least guiding the idea for a while so that they feel some involvement in the decision is helpful. Allowing them to choose sheets is helpful, too."

–SARAH PLETCHER

"I say get the big kid's bed before the child must sleep in it, and let them nap in it sometimes before making a change for nighttime sleeping."

–SUSAN LONERGAN

"When she was 2, we placed the crib with the rail down next to the bed, so she could climb back and forth between the two."

–TAMMY MCCLUSKEY, M.D.

8. What is the best way to stop thumb-sucking?

"Do it on the kid's own time. My daughter did. We told her that it was time for her to give up the bad habit and her blanket to carry around. She would be thumb-sucking with the blanket. We told her that when she went to school, other kids would not do that because it was for babies. She realized that we were right, so one day when she was 4 years old, she gave us the blanket to throw in the trash. It worked."

–CONNIE CHOATE

"Try to restrict it to only in the bedroom. If they start sucking, they go to their room."

–KARI RYDELL

"I have a thumb-sucker and he's 3 now. I was also a thumb-sucker and I didn't give it up until I was 10! Thumb-sucking is a little different and more difficult to resolve (than a pacifier) because it's attached to your hand and ready whenever you want it. You can't just take it away or throw it out. I have good days and bad with my thumb-sucking son, and I've found that if I don't call attention to it, he sucks it less. However, if I go around telling him to take his thumb out of his mouth, he sucks it more. I feel that unless the habit is causing severe problems with the teeth and speech (I don't let my son talk to me with his thumb in his mouth), you should not push your child to stop. Let him work it out on his own."

–STEPHANIE MARTIN

"I think children must outgrow this on their own. My kindergartener did not suck his thumb in school. So a child is aware, they just need to want it, too."

–LORI BURGESS

9. What is the easiest way to potty train a child?

"The absolute best way is to allow your child to do it themselves. Take a very relaxed attitude about it. They will do it when they are ready. In the initial stages of readiness, we gave our kids one M&M for 'tinkling' on the potty and two M&Ms for 'pooping' on the potty. We went shopping for big girl underpants and let the kids pick out the panties they would wear when they were all trained. Lastly, we promised one toy that my kids really wanted as a reward for when they were completely trained. Just make sure that you buy the toy in advance and hide it somewhere. We almost had a real problem because my daughter wanted a certain doll, and when she was trained, we went shopping for it, but the store didn't sell it anymore. We were fortunate to find it at another store."

–JULIE BARTLETT

"After multiple unsuccessful attempts, I got a potty video with the story about Prudence. I told my daughter to pee at the same time that Prudence went to the bathroom or, even better, to do it first."

–ELIZA LO CHIN, M.D.

"Okay, I said I would never resort to it, but we offered M&Ms and lemon treats as an enticement. My daughter was 3 years and 3 weeks old when she 'got it' and was using the potty regularly, and we stopped the candy as soon as she was going on her own."

–ANN STOWE

"Wait until they are ready. That's the best thing I know to do. Forcing a child to potty train before they are ready is useless."

–BROOKE KUHNS

"I like the idea of gradual familiarization and waiting for the child to take initiative. You can talk about the topic to steer their interest, but kids are amazing detectors of pressure on the part of the parents. I put a potty in the bathroom, but didn't make a fuss about it. He asked what it was for, I told him, no fuss, very matter-of-factly. He would occasionally sit on it (closed) and I would read him stories.

"One day, he just tried it out. After that, he went back to diapers for a while, and I didn't make any deal of that, but three months or so later, he indicated interest again. He probably started the process later than most kids (3-1/2), but there was no struggle and virtually no accidents, so in my opinion, it was worth the wait. Nighttime took a little longer, but again, when he was ready, it was smooth sailing."

–SARAH PLETCHER

CHAPTER 12:

Ready For Another One?

You've got experience on your side. But every conception, pregnancy and baby is different. And this time, you've also got one or more kids to take care of while you're pregnant. Here's how to get pregnant and enjoy it the next time around.

Our Top Four Tips When Trying to Conceive and It's Taking Longer Than Expected

1. Relax.
2. Have sex every other day.
3. Elevate your pelvis after intercourse.
4. Get help quickly.

WHY WE RECOMMEND THESE

"Try to relax! As difficult as that is, the stress you place on yourself can actually be keeping you from conceiving. Our mental state has a lot to do with the physical state of our bodies. The chemicals your body releases when stressed, anxious or depressed will interfere with your body's ability to conceive. It also helped me to remember that God had just the right baby in mind for our family. If I had become pregnant any other month, we would have had different egg and sperm and would have gotten a different baby. The three we have are just perfect for our family."

–ANGELA SNODGRASS

"We were trying for close to a year before I got pregnant, and the only thing that seems to work is the same thing that is almost impossible to do when you're actively trying to have a baby: relax, don't think about it, and just have fun. It's very true that when you stop trying is when it happens."

–K. SCARLETT SHAW

"Have intercourse every other day from day 10 to day 20 of your cycle."

–KIMBERLY MERCURIO, M.D.

"After we had intercourse, I would prop my hips up on two pillows and stay like that for 30 minutes. I did it for about two weeks, and it worked right away after two years of trying doing nothing."

–AMANDA MARBREY

"I am a big believer in not waiting if there are infertility problems, and don't let your OB (obstetrician) waste your money and use up your insurance. Go to an infertility specialist. OBs are busy doing exams, pap smears, etc. Your fertility doctor's only goal is to get you pregnant."

–ANDREA SUISSA

"It took us over a year to get pregnant, and we went through a fertility specialist. It was the month that we decided not to do all the ovulation predictors, and tried just to have fun that I finally got pregnant. I also had read somewhere that after intercourse, if you lay down for a while with your pelvis elevated that it helps the sperm move along, and we did do that the month I got pregnant."

–TRACI BRAGG, M.D.

The Top Five Ways to Take Care of Yourself When You Have Little One(s) in Tow

1. Rest as much as possible: Nap when the kids nap, and sleep when they sleep.
2. Accept help.
3. Schedule time for yourself on a regular basis.
4. Pamper yourself.
5. Spend time with the older child(ren).

WHY THIS IS IMPORTANT

"Now that I am pregnant with my third child, the best advice I can offer is to try and relax and rest when the kids are napping or watching a video. If I am rested, I can deal with everything much better. I also have a babysitter every Friday, which gives me a little alone time, and I love it."

–ANN STOWE

"Think support, whether it's family, friends, neighbors or a support group. Take time for you! It's very important to rest when you can, and always ask for help if you need it."

–ELICIA MOORE

"A great help for me, especially in the early months when I was queasy, was a 12-year-old neighbor girl. She and her friends had taken the Girl Scouts babysitter training, so if you don't know how to find a mother's helper, you might contact the Girl Scouts in your neighborhood."

—TARA TUCKER

"Schedule time to pamper yourself with small things such as an uninterrupted bubble bath. I take 'mini trips' during the week for activities no one enjoys but me!"

—DESHAWN ANDERSON

"The best way to take care of yourself when your pregnant with additional children is to eat right, get sleep when your other children rest, and don't make a Supermom out of yourself."

—TRISH HALE

"Rest as much as possible. Try playing games that don't require running (tag might not be good, but Chutes and Ladders is)."

—KAREN SULTAN

"The single most important thing to do for yourself is ask for help! You will need as much rest as you can get, and now is the perfect time to allow others to help you out with their time. Perhaps they could bring you frozen, home-prepared meals in ready-to-heat-and-serve portions. Or offer to help by taking your little one(s) off your hands for a short time, so you can get either a nap in or even get some shopping done."

—LISA BITTAR

"Hire a babysitter even if you don't want to go out. It's okay to hire a babysitter to take the kids out so you can sleep."

—DONNICA L. MOORE, M.D.

"It is so hard to get the rest that you need when you already have another child. My oldest was only 1 when we found out I was pregnant again. I had to keep up with a toddler, plus take care of myself. The best advice I can give is nap when they nap, and take advantage of whatever help you can get. I had to let a lot of housework slide in order to get the rest I needed."

—MICHELLE LANEY

"Let friends and family help as much as possible, so that you can get as much rest as possible."

—BARBARA NICHOLS

"You really need to prioritize. In other words, do only what is absolutely necessary. Older children are usually not only capable, but willing to help out. Take advantage of that."

–SALLY FARRINGTON

"Videos! Seriously, now's the time to relax your standards on TV for the kids. I never would have survived my first trimester without I Dig Dirt *and the* Teletubbies.*"*

–STACEY STEVENS

"Make time for yourself by telling the older child it's time for a nap, but if he doesn't want to sleep, he can stay in his room and play quietly."

–LAURENCE THELLIER

"Nap when they nap or have your dear husband take your older child (children) for an hour, so you can just veg or take a relaxing bath. Even a half hour will work wonders."

–BROOKE ULINSKI

"My parents used to visit a couple of times a week and give me a short break to do something special by myself (like go to the supermarket)."

–LINDA LINGUVIC

"I hired someone to come in and help me take care of my older son since he was only 3, while I was pregnant. It's a big help because sometimes you have one of those mornings where nothing is going to get you out of bed, and your husband works all day. You should make sure it's someone energetic who is able to take your kids out and do something special, should you require quiet time to sleep, especially if you're on bedrest."

–LEAH CHEW

"I continue to stay healthy by eating the correct foods, reading to the womb and playing jazz, classical music or other soothing sounds. I take them to the park, book readings and other events that will keep them occupied. I read stories to them and when they are napping, I relax, read a good book without interruptions or call friends. At other times, I arrange for a babysitter, so that I can meet my friends for lunch."

–DAWN KIRNON, M.D.

"I try to treat myself to a manicure and keep up with my hair appointments. It makes me feel more human. I also keep up with all my doctor/dentist appointments. We are all machines, and if we do not take

care of us, who will1/2 And we will break down if we don't keep up our maintenance."

–ANDREA SUISSA

"Try to take an hour each day for yourself (for exercise, bath, etc.), take offers of help from your family and friends. For an energizing drink that's healthy, make your own smoothies – it's good for you and the baby."

–BOBBI ANNAL

"Get plenty of rest, especially when the older child/ren are napping. Do not hesitate to ask for or accept help if you need it from family, friends, etc. Do not feel bad about vocalizing your needs, wants, pains, etc. to your husband."

–KELI LOVELAND

"Get plenty of rest, sleep when your other children sleep. Go for a walk with them. Try to fix them healthier snacks/meals, so you can eat healthy also."

–DEBBY MADRID

"Have your husband commit to taking care of your other children for a certain period of time each day or each week. For instance, on Saturday, plan to take 'shifts' taking care of the kids – you get a block of three hours off, and he gets a block of three hours off to do whatever you want (go out, stay home and relax, take a nap, etc.)."

–KARI RYDELL

"The early months were always the most difficult for me, since I had morning sickness. I made sure to nap while my daughter, then 1-1/2 , napped during the first trimester. One luxury I always managed to slip in was a pedicure, since I couldn't see my own feet and had two summer babies."

–KIMBERLY MERCURIO, M.D.

Breaking the News to Your Kids That a New Baby Is On the Way

TIPS FROM THE TRENCHES

✓**Keep your child(ren)'s age(s) in mind.**

"Wait as long as you can to tell them because nine months can seem like an eternity to a young child. When the new baby is born, have a gift from the baby to the sibling(s)."

—KELI LOVELAND

"Just tell them. It also helps to refer to the baby as 'our baby' to your toddler so that they get a sense of responsibility that they will help with the baby, too. It also will help them to call the new baby <toddler's name>'s baby."

—KARI RYDELL

" I told my son that I had another baby in my tummy and he would be a big brother. We told him how important the role of a big brother was. I also bought him a baby doll so he could practice feeding and holding the baby."

—DENINE SCALLEN

Meet our Contributing Authors

ALBRIGHT, ANGELA

Angela Albright is from Allentown, Pa. She loves spending time both with her two children and with her husband alone, when she has a chance. To restore her sanity, she goes for walks with her children and chats online with other moms.

ALDER, REBECCA

Rebecca Alder lives in Muskego, Wis. with her husband, Kevin, daughter, Abigail, and two beagles, and is expecting another baby soon. When she is not pulling her daughter out of the dogs' water bowl, she enjoys reading, cooking and listening to jam bands, notably Phish.

ANDERSON, DESHAWN

Deshawn Anderson is living in Apopka, Fla while completing her medical internship. When she isn't consumed with her husband, Yohannes, children, Ashley and Yahanna, and her internship, she enjoys Israeli folk dancing and geneology research. She is expecting another child later this year. Her favorite saying is, "Jesus loves you, so take time to love others."

ANDERSON, SYLVIA

Sylvia Anderson lives in Rapid City, S.D. with her husband and 3-year-old son, Adam. She is currently studying at the University of South Dakota School of Medicine and, as such, is chronically tired and always looking for shortcuts. In her spare time, she enjoys driving five hours across South Dakota to join her husband "working cows" on his family's ranch.

ANNAL, BOBBI

Spokane, Wash. is home to Bobbi Annal, her husband and two daughters. She has many interests, including crafts, scrapbooking, drawing and writing. Leisure time for her is sitting in the backyard in the early morning and drinking a cup of tea before the day gets started. She believes that having at least two hours to herself every day does amazing things for her heart and soul (not to mention the fact that it prevents her from being a dragon, since she's already had her "time-out").

ARNOLD, PATRICIA

Patricia Arnold lives in Westford, Mass. with her husband and toddler twins. She fondly remembers the days when she enjoyed reading, crafts, traveling and conversations that did not involve mention of bodily functions. Her philosophy on parenting is to pick her battles and not to sweat the small stuff.

AUTRY, ELAINE

Elaine Autry lives in Chicago, Ill. with her son, Cody (1 year) and husband, John. By participating in this book, she hopes to share the knowledge she's just beginning to stumble upon.

BARTLETT, JULIE

Julie Bartlett lives in Bettendorf, Iowa with her husband, Jon, and two children, Eliza and Sarah. She enjoys volunteering at her church and her children's school. She is also active in the local chapter of Mothers of Preschoolers (MOPS). Her favorite leisure time activities are reading, sewing and doing crafts.

BEDROSIAN, DIANE

Pediatrician Diane Bedrosian, M.D., lives with her husband and two girls, ages 3-1/2 and 18 months, in Carlsbad, Calif. A fellow of the American Academy of Pediatrics, she has been in private practice for ten years and is currently working part-time, so she can spend more time with her children. When not running around with her kids, she enjoys running at the beach and volunteering at a local cat spay-neuter organization.

BEZENEK, TESSICA

Tessica Bezenek lives in Salt Lake City, Utah with her son, Jayden, and her Shih Tzu (dog), Dakota. Her favorite pastimes are reading, cooking and watching her son explore the world. She maintains her sanity by spending time with her family and surfing the Internet.

BIENVENU, CLAIRE

Slidell, La. is home to Claire Bienvenu, her husband, Frank Spiess, and their baby, Vivienne. A licensed professional counselor and college administrator, Claire enjoys spending time with family and friends, cooking, dining out, reading, gardening and dancing. She is hopeful that these activities will resume with more regularity soon.

BITTAR, LISA

Single mom Lisa Bittar (a.k.a. Superwoman) is raising her three awesome children: Timothy Joseph, Tyler Dylan and Madyson Rene, in Brooklyn, N.Y. For her, instilling traditions and family values in the children are what's most important. In her spare time (a mom has spare time?), she enjoys reading, listening to music and family game night with the kids.

BLECHERMAN, BETH

Menlo Park, Calif. is home to Beth Blecherman, her son, Benjamin and husband, Neil. She enjoys spending time with her family and friends and has fun with her part-time job at a work/life balance-friendly accounting firm. Her favorite leisure activity used to be reading fiction and exercising. Now she reads parenting books and gets her exercise trying to keep up with her 3-1/2 -year-old son on hikes (hikes around the neighborhood, hikes around the park, hikes around the house....).

BRAGG, TRACI

Traci Bragg, M.D., is mother to twin 4-month-old boys, Nicholas and Matthew. She lives with her sons and her husband, Brad, in Jacksonville, Fla., where she also works as a family medicine physician. She enjoys sewing and crafts, taking walks with the family, playing with the boys as much as possible and going to the mall, where she is stopped at least 15 times with the comment, "Oh how cute. Are they twins?"

BRIGHT, KEL

Charleston Air Force Base is home to Kel Bright, her husband, Tech. Sgt. Michael Bright, and their son, Ashton. Ashton is a playful little boy who never slows down, while Kel and Michael just try to take things one day at a time.

BROWN, BRENDA

Montclair, Va.-based Brenda Brown spends her days with a toddler who seems bent on trying to make her run the gamut of emotions from frustration to adoration. After years of working in a classroom full of 2-year-olds, she is amazed how far one precocious child can stretch her creative boundaries on a daily basis. She spends her leisure time learning more about attachment-parenting and child development.

BURGESS, LORI

Maine is home to Lori Burgess, who enjoys raising her four children and living life fully through their eyes. When not carpooling and tackling laundry, she is in her garden or lounging by the pool. In the cold winter months, there is always hot soup simmering in the pot, while the family enjoys winter pastimes together.

CAMPAGNA, SARAH E.

21-year-old Sarah E. Campagna lives in Uncasville, Conn. with her husband and 1-year-old son. She enjoys cooking and reading. She works part-time at night and chases her nutty baby around all day! Her favorite thing to do is to sleep.

CARLON, MICHELE F.

Michele Carlon, M.D., is a general internist. She and her husband, Juan R. Herena, M.D., have two children, Tommy, 3-1/2 , and Ellie, 18 months. She is presently working to purchase her practice from the hospital where she is currently employed in Oak Park, Ill. Balancing motherhood and the busy life of a practicing physician is quite a task, and she relies heavily on good child-care. She has a come and go "teacher caregiver," who is terrific.

CHARLES, BRANDY

Tulsa, Okla.-based Brandy Charles is a new mom who enjoys spending her free time with her son and husband. In addition, she enjoys being outdoors and loves life now that her son sleeps for more than four hours at a time. Her favorite quote is, "Rest? What's that?"

CHEW, LEAH

Leah Chew lives in Tucker, Ga. with her two sons, Kieran and Onan, and her wonderful, helping husband, Frank. She enjoys sewing, cooking, sleeping, reading and performing *The Rocky Horror Picture Show* on Fridays.

CHIN, ELIZA LO

Eliza Lo Chin, M.D., is a doctor of internal medicine, who lives in Piedmont, Calif. with her husband, Douglas Chin, M.D., and their three children. She recently edited the anthology, *This Side of Doctoring: Reflections from Women in Medicine* (Sage Publications, 2002), a project that grew out of her interest in the challenges that women face when balancing career and family. She currently practices medicine part-time and devotes the remainder of her time to her children and her writing.

CHOATE, CONNIE

The proud, deaf mom of hearing children who speak sign language, Connie Choate lives in Gardner, Kan. with her four kids and her husband, Jeff. In her free time, she enjoys cooking and traveling.

CHOW, HANNAH

Elmhurst, Ill. is home to pediatrician Hannah Chow, M.D., her husband and two sons. In her past life, she enjoyed foreign travel. Currently she enjoys spending her free time with her family, reading books and travelling domestically.

CLEVELAND, JENNIFER

Jennifer Cleveland lives in Ramona, Calif. with her husband, John, and son, Christopher. She believes that a Christ-centered home is the foundation for a happy family. Cooking, reading and, most of all, spending time with her wonderful husband and son are what she enjoys most. Her best piece of parenting advice is, "Cherish every moment with your children. They are only little for a short time, and you can't turn back the hands of time!"

COCCHIOLA, HOLLY

Holly Cocchiola lives in Bethlehem, Conn. with her husband, Ray, and little darling, Liam. In her spare time (ha, ha), she eats, sleeps and breathes. She loves being a stay-at-home mom, as well as photography and being at the beach.

COFFEY HAMMAN, CHELSEA

Chelsea Coffey Hamman lives in Providence, N.C. with her daughter, Faith, and husband, Jonathan. Being a busy medical student, she enjoys spending her precious free time with her family doing "anything and everything that doesn't involve a hospital."

CONROY, KATHLEEN

Kathleen Conroy resides in Palos Hills, Ill. with her husband, Mike and 15-month-old son, Brendan. Formerly a preschool teacher, she now enjoys staying home with her son.

CROY, DANA A.

Murfreesboro, TN is home to Dana Croy, her husband, Nathan, and infant son, Noah. She is a stay-at-home mom who works part time for a metaphysical bookstore. In her free time, she works on expanding her consciousness and her connection with God and the Goddess. She is currently writing two books: a wedding planner and a recipe book. She hopes to pass on her creativity and spirituality to her son in a stable and structured environment.

CURTIS, REBECCA

Rebecca Curtis lives in Oshawa, Ontario, Canada with her husband, Albert, and children, Zachary and Savannah. She enjoys playing the flute and saxophone, watching hockey, and going yard sale shopping. Her parenting philosophy is, "It isn't about luck in parenting, birth or hockey. It's about skill and patience. And a little pain tolerance never hurt either."

DAVIDSON, DONNA

Weymouth, Mass. is home to Donna Davidson, her daughter and husband, Don. She enjoys sunny days, spending time with her family and reading. The wonder and excitement children possess and create in their environment truly amazes her. She says, "Having a child is like witnessing life for the first time all over again."

DINTIMAN, BRENDA

Working full-time as a dermatologist since 1991, Brenda Dintiman, M.D., has been running her own private practice in Fairfax, Va. since 1994. She has two children, Christine, 12, and Teddy, 9, who are active in soccer, chorus and Odyssey of the Mind. Married to a financial consultant, Ted Shanahan, she is an avid tennis player, gardener and very active in her children's activities and school.

DIXON, SARA

Sara Dixon lives in Grimesland, N.C. with her husband Mark. They have five children and two dogs. She works full-time as a nurse. She adores her husband and children, and wouldn't trade them for anything, except maybe a little peace and quiet. Her current motto is "Sanity is for wimps."

DOBRATZ, SUSAN

Susan Dobratz lives with her daughter and husband in Plymouth, Mass. She enjoys her new role as a mother and has chosen to be a stay-at-home mom. Walking and reading are two of the ways she has found to escape the crazy days of motherhood.

DOUGLAS, WENDY

Wendy Douglas lives in Margate, Fla. with her husband and three little men. She enjoys spending time with her family and friends. The best advice she can give is, "Don't sweat the small stuff. And remember that 2 doesn't last forever...there is always 3, 4, 5...well, you get the idea!"

DRAGONETTI, LORI

Lori Dragonetti has three children. She lives in North Haledon, N.J.

EVANS, BARBARA

Arvada, Colo. is home to Barbara Evans, her five daughters and husband, Scott. They love going to car shows and showing their 1923 Model T. She keeps her sanity by working part-time and scrapbooking. She also enjoys being with her two retired greyhounds, Gabby and Zelda.

FARRINGTON, SALLY

Sally Farrington lives in Fayetteville, N.C. with her three beautiful daughters and military husband, Dave. They have homeschooled their children for eight years and really enjoy the closeness that it has allowed. She enjoys reading, gardening, church and hugging her girls!

FRENCH, HEATHER

Heather French lives in Noblesville, Ind. with her husband, Jason, and their miracle son, Liam. She loves spending time with her son, as she endured nine years of infertility before having him. When he allows her free time, she enjoys playing with her digital photography software.

GANE, JESSICA

Brookhaven, Pa. is home to Jessica Gane and her daughter. She spends her free time fire-fighting and doing ambulance work. When she needs a break (usually twice a week), her dad watches the baby. If it weren't for family, friends and her wonderful boyfriend, Phil, she wouldn't have made it this far.

GASTON, BECKY

Becky Gaston lives in Owensboro, Ky. with her daughter, Haleigh Marie, and husband, Nathan. She enjoys taking long walks with her toddler and taking her to the zoo and the pool. She is also a full-time law student. Becky's favorite activity is cuddle time with Haleigh.

GEBHARD, MICHELLE

Emergency Medicine Resident Michelle Gebhard, D.O., lives in White Plains, NY with her 6-month-old daughter, Sabine and husband, Kai, her greatest ally in this hectic world. She tries to find something great about every scenario, especially whatever it is that has her complaining the most. That way, she's part of a solution instead of the problem.

GOOD, ANITA

Anita Good lives in Bloomfield, N.J. with her husband, Charlie, and her son, Ryan. She enjoys reading, writing and playing with Ryan.

GREENWOOD, DENISE

Denise Greenwood, M.D., is a native Texan, living in Little Rock, AR. She is the mother of two awesome little guys, Ford, 6, and Tucker, 4. A breast surgeon, she hung up a solo shingle in order to allow herself the freedom to raise her little ones in her office (with the help of her mother) as time permitted. They each have their own little white coats and are now listening to heart sounds and helping excise benign lumps and bumps! The littlest one has been know to apologize for his mother's work, though. "I'm so sorry my mother cut you," he'll say. Though medicine has become tough, Denise encourages it as a profession in a heartbeat. She says, "I can't think of a better way to make a living!"

GUAY, SHANNON

Shannon Guay lives in Galloway, Ohio with her husband, Christopher, and their two children. She currently works part-time and enjoys reading, listening to music and looking for fun and exciting ways for her family to spend time together.

HAAS, KAREN

Karen Haas lives in Laurel, Md. with her two children and her husband, Mark. She enjoys entertaining friends and family at her home, vacationing at the beach and attending her children's many sporting events. Her favorite leisure-time activity is soaking in a hot bubble bath when the kids are off to sleep.

HALE, TRISH

Trish Hale lives in Hanover, Md. with her husband, Mike, and their two kids, Matt and Bethany. She enjoys spring planting, collecting angels and nature. She especially likes to go to the beach on vacation with her family.

HALLBERG, KATE

Kate Hallberg lives in Boulder, Colo. with her three children, husband, Dirk Grunwald, her dear dog, Dakota, and three cats. While nursing the youngest, a happy toddler, she reads a lot, especially child development literature, an occasional breastfeeding or childbirth book and lots of novels. She enjoys hiking and skiing (of course), gardening (such as it is in Colo.), cooking in her newly-remodeled kitchen and brewing beer. She's trying to figure out what she'll do when she grows up — lactation consultant, teacher at her children's School of Excellence or return to small animal physiology? She is the web mistress of one of the top 100 linked web sites on breastfeeding: www.cs.colorado.edu/~kolina/advantages-of-formula.html.

HAMMONTREE, SARA

Sara Hammontree lives in Mountain Home, Ark. with her son, Joseph. She is enjoying this time as a full-time mom before returning to school to study law. She likes to spend her free time crafting and bargain-hunting.

HARDEN, KELLY

Kelly Harden lives in Fort Hood, Texas with her son and husband. She enjoys spending time with her family, dancing and scrapbooking. Her favorite leisure-time activity is napping, then waking up to her son's smile.

HARPER, REBECCA

Rhode Island native Rebecca Harper currently lives in Gaston, S.C. with her significant other, Art. She works part-time alongside Art in his business, and spends every other available moment with their two sons, Michael and Jordan. Her favorite leisure-time activities are reading and sleeping, although with a toddler and an infant, she doesn't get much time for anything other than being mommy.

HENDRICKSON, HEATHER

Heather Hendrickson lives in Yucaipa, Calif. with her husband, Nick, and 14-month-old son, Chance. She enjoys spending time with her family, redecorating her house and going to local MOMS Club functions.

HOSSZU, STEPHANIE

Stephanie Hosszu lives in Vancouver, Wash. with her daughter, Brynna, and husband, John. She enjoys spending time with her family, being active in her church and volunteering as the children's leader for her local MOPS program. In addition, she likes to scrapbook, stamp and read when she has free time.

HULAN, RACHEL

Rachel Hulan lives in Lake Forest, Calif. with her husband, Ron, and their 7-month-old son. She finds motherhood to be the most wonderful job she's ever had.

HUNLEY, JAMIE

Jamie Hunley lives in San Diego, Calif. with her husband, Michael, daughter Skylar, two dogs, three cats, a rabbit and a bird. She is currently working as a stay-at-home mom. Her favorite parenting advice is, "Don't listen to anyone else's advice. Just throw out your preconceived notions, and do what works best for your family. Every child and every family is different; you need to trust your own instincts and be true to yourself."

HURST, KAREN

Roseville, Calif. is home to Karen Hurst, her beautiful daughter, and husband of 10 years. She enjoys spending time with her family, scrapbooking, cross-stitching and painting — when her daughter and three cats let her!

JOHNSON, ANNA MARIA

Anna Maria Johnson resides in Shreveport, La. with her husband, Mike, and her baby boy, Thomas Payne. She enjoys exercising, scrapbooking and spending time with her family. "I love being a mom," she says, "It is the best feeling in the world looking into your baby's eyes for the first time and seeing the affection he has for you. It's a feeling that is etched in your heart forever."

JUDICE, BRANDI

Brandi Judice lives in New Iberia, La. with her three children.

KIRNON, DAWN

Oncologist Dawn Kirnon, M.D., lives in New York City with her three daughters and her king – er, husband — Albert. She enjoys spending time with her family, hosting slumber parties, touring the city museums and restaurant-hopping. Her favorite leisure-time activity is taking an uninterrupted bubble bath and fantasizing about the Caribbean.

KISTLER, MARI

Stay-at-home mom Mari Kistler lives in hot and humid St. Petersburg, Fla. with her husband, Nathan, and her son. She enjoys thinking of what she would do if she had more free time, as well as keeping her local Starbucks in business. Her plans are to return to school soon to pursue a degree in early education to become a teacher by the time her son goes off to school himself.

KOSEC, MICHELLE

Michelle Kosec lives in Glen Burnie, Md. with her son, Alexander. She enjoys many activities with him, such as swinging at the park and splashing in the pool. When she's not busy being a mom, she enjoys reading good books and writing in her journal.

KUHNS, BROOKE

Brooke Kuhns resides in Dayton, Ohio with her three boys and her husband, Sean. She enjoys cross-stitching, Stephen King novels and good movies (not that she ever gets to do any of those things with three little ones, but she remembers that they were fun).

LANE, SABRINA

Sabrina Lane lives in Boise, Idaho with her husband, David, and her two beautiful daughters, Mercedes and Tapanga. In her free time, she can be found curled up on the couch with a good book. "I love being a mom," she says. "I have these two little lives to mold, and I pray every night that I raise them right."

LANEY, MICHELLE

Michelle Laney lives in Helena, Ala. with her husband, David, and their two daughters. She has a degree in marketing, but right now is enjoying being a stay-at-home mom.

LAURIN, CHANTAL

Chantal Laurin enjoys spending time teaching her 5-month-old daughter, Erika, new things. They especially like listening to music and dancing around the house. They live in Concord, Ontario, Canada with her husband Jeff, who just can't get enough of his pretty little girl. They cannot imagine life without her!

LICHTENFELD, SHARON

Born in London, England, Sharon Lichtenfeld now lives in Atherton, Calif. and doesn't miss the English weather at all. With her husband and son, she enjoys spending weekends in San Francisco (except when it's foggy) and trying all the great restaurants. She is still trying to get over the fact that she has become a typical suburban mom.

LINGUVIC, LINDA

New York City-based Linda Linguvic has three grown children and two young grandchildren. She writes a daily e-mail column about books, movies, current events and anything that happens to interest her, such as her 2-year-old grandson who has already (to her delight) mastered using a computer mouse.

LONERGAN, SUSAN

Susan Lonergan resides in Woodside, Calif. with her two children who are under the age of 4, two children who are in college, and a very wise husband who, after having four children, is an expert in being a "mommy," too.

LONGENBACH, MICHELE

Michele Longenbach lives in Garden Grove, Calif. with her husband, Roger, and son, Robbie. She is active in a local MOMS club and works part-time from home as a medical transcriptionist. She is an avid reader and Internet fanatic, and enjoys playing The Sims while Robbie is napping.

LOVELAND, KELI

Memphis, Tenn.-based Keli Loveland is the energetic mother of three girls. She loves to play softball and knows everything there is to know about computers. When not busy running around with her girls, she can be found surfing the Net or relaxing with her husband, David.

LUCIER, NICOLE

Nicole Lucier lives in Chatham, Ontario, Canada with her husband, Chris, and their son. Now that she has a baby, she has a whole new respect for all mothers. "Just when you think you've got your little one all figured out, he up and changes on you," she says. "It's a very busy, full-time job. But it is the most rewarding job you'll ever have."

MACZKO, HEATHER

Heather Maczko is a full-time mom of two with a background in early childhood education. She lives in Beford, Mass. During her free time she enjoys spending time with friends and family, scrapbooking and shopping.

MADDEN, SHERYL

Sheryl Madden lives in Lake Forest Park, Wash. with her two boys, Ryan, 18, and Bryce, 3, and her husband, Jerry. She loves being a stay-at-home mom and is more relaxed about child-rearing "this time around." Her leisure time is spent cross-stitching or being online with friends.

MADRID, DEBBY

Elkhart, Ind. is home to Debby Madrid, her two children and husband. She enjoys being a stay-at-home mom and taking care of her family. Her favorite leisure-time activity is spending time with her family and taking them on outings.

MARBREY, AMANDA

Amanda Marbrey, husband, Michael, and daughter, Alexis Faith, live in Dyersburg, Tenn. In her spare time she enjoys going for walks, fishing or doing something quiet and peaceful with her husband. During family time, she enjoys watching Disney cartoons.

MARION-DOYLE, DANIELLE

Danielle Marion-Doyle lives in Donaldsonville, La. with her two children and her husband, Tim. Crocheting, reading and spending time with her family are some of her favorite activities. She is also a former Language Arts teacher and is currently homeschooling her children.

MARKS, SIDNEY

Sidney Marks lives in Menlo Park, Calif. with her husband, their three children and the family dog. She is a stay-at-home mom and thrives on the chaos of family life with three little ones age 3 and younger.

MARTIN, STEPHANIE

Stephanie Martin lives in Macomb, Mich. with her husband, Lynn, and three children, Philip (4), William (3), and Lillian (10 months). This super busy, ultra-organized, no-nonsense stay-at-home mother can be found diving into the latest mystery novel, cooking or crafting when she's not tending to her greatest joy — her family.

MARTIN, MEGAN

Megan Martin, age 33, lives in Crystal Lake, Ill. with her husband, Lance, and daughter, Halle. Megan is a stay-at-home mom who loves working part-time from home creating marketing and promotional pieces for a leading local real estate company. Megan is a firm believer in the adage, "the only perfect parent is the one without children!"

MATH, KRISTEN

Sartell, Minn. is home to Kristen Math, her three children, an Australian Shepherd, and her husband, Thomas. She is the founder of medicalspouse.org, a web site community providing support to the spouses of physicians. She also speaks fluent German and enjoys reading and bike-riding.

MCCANN, NINA

Nina McCann lives in Berwyn, Ill. with her husband, Tom, and their daughter. She enjoys reading, going to the movies and going out with friends.

MCCLUSKEY, TAMMY

Kinnelon, N.J.-based mom, Tammy McCluskey, M.D., works part-time in her current pediatric medical practice in order to participate actively in the lives of her two young children, ages 8 and 4.

MCCONNELL, APRIL

April McConnell and her husband, Mark, have two children, Taylor Paige and Ethan Brady. They live in Birdsboro, Pa. She works full-time as a legal secretary and enjoys shopping (for her children, of course) and spending time with her family.

MCDONALD, LISA

Lisa McDonald lives in Maitland, Fla. with her husband, Andy, and son, Maximilian. She is a firm believer that in order to be a caring, loving parent, a person must have patience and respect for her child. She likes to spend her leisure time playing on the Internet and taking long, hot bubble baths to relax at night. Whenever she has a bad day at work, she looks at her son, and no matter what, he always makes her smile.

MEININGER, HEATHER

Heather Meininger resides in Charlotte, N.C. with her daughter and husband, Kevin. She enjoys playing with her daughter, working with the fourth and fifth grade drama group at her church and working on her web site. In her spare time (when she gets any!), she enjoys crafts and is currently learning how to knit.

MERCURIO, KIMBERLY

Kimberly Mercurio, M.D. is currently a stay-at-home mom residing in Downers Grove, Ill, with her husband, Jim, and three children. She enjoys scrapbooking, reading and playing tennis when she is not chauffeuring, nursing or playing kitchen. She plans to return to the practice of medicine when her youngest child begins grade school.

MILES, MEGAN

Megan Miles lives in Marysville, Wash. with her husband Dave, her 11-year-old son and her 3-year-old daughter. Her days are filled with a high-energy toddler, a busy middle-schooler and a great career as a Tupperware manager. Eventually, she aspires to be a midwife, doula or lactation consultant. In the meantime, she loves the chaos that is her life.

MILLER, BETH

Beth Miller lives in Novato, Calif. with her son, Sam, and husband, Steve. She and Sam love going for walks everyday with friends, because fresh air can make a world of difference for a stressed-out mom and baby. Her favorite parenting tip is, "Trust yourself. No one knows your kids better than you do."

MOLLOY, GENEVIEVE

Genevieve Molloy is a stay-at-home mom who lives with her daughter, Sophia, and husband, Tommy, in Guttenberg, N.J. Having worked in the fashion field for over ten years, she believes that staying home with her daughter has been the most gratifying experience of her life.

MOORE, DONNICA L.

Obstetrician/Gynocologist Donnica Moore, M.D., resides in Neshanic Station, N.J. and is a highly-regarded expert on women's health. A physician educator and media commentator, she has appeared on more than 300 television and radio shows, including NBC's *Weekend Today*. She has also been featured in articles in *The New York Times, The Washington Post, Business Week* and *The Wall Street Journal*. She is the founder and president of DrDonnica.com, a popular women's health information web site. She is also the founder and president of Sapphire Women's Health Group, a multimedia women's health education and communications firm. Most importantly, she is the mother of two school-aged children who have taught her much more about the importance of health and wellness than all of her medical training.

MOORE, ELICIA

Elicia Moore lives in Monrovia, Calif. with her husband, Brian, and their three daughters', Kayla, Makaele, and Autumn. She enjoys volunteering at her kids' school, spending time with her family and reading. Her favorite leisure-time activity is locking the bathroom door and soaking in a hot bubble bath.

NICHOLS, BARBARA

Barbara Nichols resides in Okeechobee, Fla. with her husband and three children, ages 1 to 18. She enjoys spending time with her family and volunteering at her church. Her favorite leisure-time activity is going to the water theme park and watching her children ride the slides.

OESTERREICHER, LAMIEL

Lamiel Oesterreicher resides in Brooklyn, N.Y. and is currently a stay-at-home mom to her beautiful daughter, Maya Rose. When she's not feeding or entertaining her baby girl, she likes to spend her free time taking hot showers and catching up on some much-needed sleep.

PALMER, DEBBIE

Debbie Palmer lives in Hickory, N.C. with her two sons and husband, Lewis. She enjoys spending time with her family, working in the church nursery, cooking and sewing. Her favorite leisure-time activity is introducing her children to the world of Medieval Reenactment.

PARKS, LYNN

Lynn Parks lives with her husband and son in Durham, N.C. She is active in the PTA and volunteers in her son's classroom. Her interests include reading and painting.

PARO, STACI

Staci Paro lives in Massachusetts with her two children, Joshua and Julia, and her husband, Jon. She enjoys family picnics at the park, long Sunday drives and walking in the woods. Her favorite leisure-time activity is a hot bath with bubbles, candles and, of course, chocolate! Staci firmly believes that organization and routine is essential when it comes to infants and toddlers.

PLETCHER, SARAH

East Lansing, Mich. is home to Sarah Pletcher and her son Henry, age 4. She is entering her third year of medical school and is jointly completing a Master's degree. In her spare time (ha!), she plays competitive tennis. She tells Henry every night that she must be the luckiest mama in the whole world to have him for a son.

PLODZIEN, ERIKA

Erika Plodzien lives in Plainfield, Ill. with her daughter, Calista, and husband, Stan. She enjoys taking small trips with the family and gardening. In her spare time, she tries to watch a movie or read a book.

PRICE, TIFFANY K.

Tiffany K. Price lives in Vancouver, Canada with her son, Jack, and husband, John. She says, "I have always felt 'in control' of my life and was confident that, if confronted with anything I was not sure about, I could research it and find the answers. Having Jack has been a wonderful life lesson. I am blissfully in control of nothing." She is the vice president of business development for a software firm and enjoys the flexibility of being able to work from her home office.

PRINCE, TAMARA

Tamara Prince is a counselor who lives in Oshawa, Ontario, Canada with her daughter and husband. Her hobbies include scrapbooking, hiking and running. She also enjoys spending a lot of her spare time with her extended family, and is very concerned about children's safety, especially when it comes to car seats and toys.

PRITCHARD, TRACY

Tracy Pritchard lives in Kyle, Texas with her three children and husband, Matt. She enjoys spending time with her family, sewing, scrapbooking and reading. Finishing more than one page of a book at a time — without interruption — is her current quest!

RAB, KRISZTINA

Krisztina Rab resides in Naperville, Ill. with her husband and son. She works in Chicago as a tax attorney and is the founder and treasurer of the Nyul Foundation, a charity that raises money for the medical expenses of cancer patients. She especially enjoys bath time with her son and plans to have him swimming by 2 years of age, in the hope that this will burn off some of his seemingly inexhaustible energy. She firmly believes in giving children a ton of affection and lots of playtime with their parents, and attributes her son's good sleeping and eating habits to this philosophy (whether rightly or wrongly is open for discussion).

REICH, CHAYA JAMIE

Chaya Jamie Reich lives in Los Angeles with her daughter, Adele, and her husband, Gideon. She believes that a child's education begins at home. When not being a devoted wife and mother, she enjoys the fine arts and classical literature.

RENNIE, SHERRY

Sherry Rennie resides in Rialto, Calif. with her two sons (ages 2 and 4) and her husband of seven years. She is a committed stay-at-home mom and enjoys her menagerie of pets that include a dog, cat, rats, reptiles and a fish. Her hobbies include gardening, taking pictures of her boys and scrapbooking. A good day consists of cleaning up less that 200 messes and not having to say, "Don't pee on your brother."

RIVERA-ROGERS, MONIQUE

Monique Rivera-Rogers is the bilingual, stay-at-home parent of a nursing toddler. Her family believes in vegetarianism, attachment parenting and living a socially-conscious lifestyle. They enjoy cross-country travel and visiting with their extended families. She and her husband, Ryan, are rearing their son, Aidan, to understand that support from family and friends is vital in getting through life's challenges.

ROSE, JENNIFER

Jennifer Rose lives in Boston with her husband, Eric, and 1-year-old daughter, Rebecca (and a brother or sister on the way). She balances work, a Master's class and parenting, and looks forward to the summer when she can finally get out of the classroom and onto the softball field. Since Rebecca came along, things have certainly changed, but luckily they haven't all stopped.

RYDELL, KARI

Kari Rydell lives in Ladera Ranch, Calif. with her husband and son. She enjoys playing the piano, shopping (especially for and with the new baby) and cleaning (really!). Her former life as a computer programmer is still showing, as she has now switched gears from software engineering to writing little programs to chart and graph the baby's sleeping and eating schedules.

SADIKMAN, CAREN

Caren Sadikman, M.D., lives in Rochester, Minn. with her husband and her daughter, Sophia. She believes in showering children with hugs, love and attention. She is a resident physician in Physical Medicine and Rehabilitation and enjoys winding down at the end of the day by playing with Sophie, watching her taped soap opera and eating ice cream. She also believes in giving her husband plenty of time to play golf and fish in between diaper changes!

SCALLEN, DENINE

Denine Scallen is a stay-at-home mom who lives in Sammamish, Wash. with her husband and two sons. Her favorite activities are teaching her children to cook, painting and jewelry making. She looks forward to one day leading a life free of changing diapers.

SCHISSER, DIANNA

Dianna Schisser lives in Leander, Texas with her son, Marq, and husband, Trey. She enjoys spending time with her friends and family, volunteering at the local MOMS club and staying at home with her son. Her favorite leisure activities are photography, scrapbooking and stamping.

SHAW, K. SCARLETT

K. Scarlett Shaw is a stay-at-home mom living in Euless, Texas with her husband, Brad, and their 11-month-old son, Sam. She enjoys going to the park and flying kites, reading to her son — and herself — and crafting. She would someday like to be an early childhood education teacher.

SHOULTS, CRYSTAL

Linn, MO is home to Crystal Shoults, her four kids, Cody, Tyler, Brianna and Garrett, and her husband, Ronnie. She enjoys trading items on the Internet and spending time with her family. Her favorite leisure-time activity is watching her kids play and have fun. Her philosophy on raising kids is, "Every child has their own personality."

SKLAR, STACEY
Stacey Sklar lives in Oakland, Calif. with her husband, Eugene Hahm, and their daughter, Madeline. She teaches high school English, and enjoys theater, running and the outdoors.

SMEAD, THERESA
The proud wife of a U.S. Army officer, Theresa Smead is a stay-at-home/work-from-home mom of boy/girl twins. Her family is currently stationed in St. Louis, Mo., allowing them to live close to her parents in St. Peters, Mo., and this has been both a comfort and a blessing. She believes her struggle with infertility changed her and affected the way she later parented her children. While she does not follow any one parenting philosophy, she has embraced many of the child-centered attachment parenting philosophies to include breastfeeding and child-wearing. She remembers cross-stitching and writing poetry as hobbies, but lately finds herself more amused with *Blue's Clues* and *Dora the Explorer*, a testament, she believes, to the joy of participating in a child's growth and learning.

SMITH, STEPHANIE R.
Stephanie R. Smith, her three children and husband, Rob, live in Alexandria, Ky. She tries to remind herself on a daily basis to keep a somewhat relaxed parenting style. She wants to guide her kids, not smother them. Her favorite leisure-time activity is spending a day with her kids doing what they want and then having time leftover at the end of the day with her husband.

SNODGRASS, ANGELA
Angela Snodgrass lives in Meridian, Idaho with her husband, Michael, and their three active little boys. She is a homeschooling mom who enjoys scrapbooking, reading and having tea with friends.

SOLOMON HUGGINS, SHELLY
Shelly Solomon Huggins, Ed.D., lives in Bel Air, Md. She adores her loving husband, Matt, and her remarkable daughter, Kirstin. Her husband and she focus their family decisions and activities around God-centered values. She has a doctorate in education and works as a full-time achievement facilitator for a local public school system. As a working mother, she spends every free moment enjoying her family at home. She has had the blessing of having an amazing mommy herself and is so grateful for her own parents' influence on her life.

STEGER, JODI
Jodi Steger lives in Jersey City, N.J. with her husband, Lon, and 16-month-old daughter, Neve. She loves being a stay-at-home mom, and focuses on surrounding Neve with a ton of love (hugs, kisses and miles of smiles). Neve seems to be benefiting from this approach because she is truly always smiling!

STEIN, RIVKA
Rivka Stein, M.D., is a pediatric resident in Brooklyn, N.Y. Her favorite leisure activity is spending time with her husband and three children, ages 5, 2 and 6 months.

STEIMAN, KATE

Kate Steiman is a British import, now living in Toms River, N.J. with her American husband and two American children. Though she enjoys the chaos of having two children 22 months apart, her favorite leisure-time activity is watching something other than *Barney* on TV.

STEVENS, STACEY

Stacey Stevens lives in Alamo, Calif. with her husband and two small boys. Before having kids, Stacey was a management consultant and failed "dot-commer" who enjoyed skiing, reading and roller-coasters. Now she would give anything for a good night's sleep like she used to get during her 100-hour work weeks!

STINSON-WESLEY, AMELIA

Amelia Stinson-Wesley is a first-time mom who lives in Morganton, N.C. with her husband and daughter. An ordained minister and human rights activist, she works with women around the world who have been victims of interpersonal violence. However, being a mother is the most challenging and fulfilling job she's ever had.

STOWE, ANN

Ann Stowe lives in Burlingame, Calif. with her two children and husband, Nick. They are happily anticipating the arrival of their third child in November. She enjoys spending time with her family and friends.

STUSSIE, LORI

Lori Stussie is based in Lawrence, Kan. with her three sons and husband, Larry. She loves her job teaching English in an alternative high school and coaching athletics. In her spare time, she loves to scrapbook and may soon need to start a chapter of Scrapbookers Anonymous if she cannot quit spending her paycheck on supplies! Other favorite hobbies include reading and participating in sports.

SUISSA, ANDREA

Andrea Suissa lives in Olney, Md. with her husband, Dan, sons Alec (5), twins Chase and Chad (2-1/2) and daughter Samantha (13-months). She enjoys every free moment she can get! For fun, she likes being online, chatting with friends and doing activities with her children.

SULTAN, KAREN

Karen Sultan lives in Rockville, Md. with her husband, David, their three boys, Jamey (6), Noah (3), and Coby (13 months) and two cats. She is currently on leave from her position as an English teacher in Montgomery County. During her free time, she enjoys reading, cooking and walking.

TACHNA, SUSAN

Palo Alto, Calif. is home to Susan Tachna, her two sons and her husband, Steve. She spends her time chasing her two boys around, making sure that everyone is well fed, clothed, bathed and tickled. She enjoys reading, hiking, cooking, traveling and — most of all – spending time with her family and friends.

THELLIER, LAURENCE

Laurence Thellier is a stay-at-home mom living in Kyoto, Japan with her husband and two girls. She enjoys family time, traveling, cooking and learning Japanese whenever the kids let her.

THERIAULT, DEBORAH

Ocean Springs, Miss. is home to Deborah Theriault, her daughter and husband. She enjoys horseback riding and getting outdoors. Her favorite saying in life is, "Just roll with it."

TUCKER, TARA

Tara Tucker lives in Mountain View, Calif. with her husband, David, and children, Katie and Michael. Connecting with the local Las Madres MOMS group has kept her sane since she left a professional career two years ago to become a full-time mom.

ULINSKI, BROOKE

Brooke Ulinski is a stay-at-home mom in Levittown, Pa. She and her husband, Mike, have two young sons and an infant daughter. She enjoys playing with her children and watching them run around like crazy in the backyard.

VANCE, LORI

Lori Vance lives in Huntington Beach, Calif. with her husband and their girl/boy twins.

VICARS DOWNS, VALERIE

Valerie Vicars Downs is a stay-at-home mom living in Altoona, Pa. with her son, Alexander, and husband, Jason. In her spare time, she likes to read and talk to other mothers.

VINCENS, CARA

Cara Vincens is a Canadian mom living in France with her husband, Matthieu, and their son, Jacques. Besides spending time with her boys, she loves scrapbooking, reading and running. Her husband often teases her for having read every book ever written on parenting, but when it comes down to it, she tends to follow her gut. She says, "It always knows best!"

WEAVER, COLLEEN GRACE

Colleen Grace Weaver lives in Magalia, Calif. She is a licensed day care provider and owner of Weaver Infant Day Care. She practices attachment parenting with her daughter.

WILSON, KAREN

Karen Wilson lives in Fairport, N.Y. with her husband and two children, ages 6 and 8. She is a full-time medical student at the University of Rochester, and eventually hopes to be in academic medicine. Right now she is just trying to make it through her third year.

WILSON, VERONICA

Veronica Wilson is a 24-year-old pediatric nursing student who lives in Chattanooga, Tenn. with her two sons, ages 6 and 6 months. She loves and respects her children and follows her heart when it comes to parenting. She believes in tending to her children's needs quickly and always letting them know she is there for them. She doesn't spank her son or let her infant "cry it out." Instead, she prefers attachment-style parenting. Loving her children and seeing their happiness is enough to make her feel that everything she has done works just perfectly.

WONDERLING, JULIE

Julie Wonderling lives outside of Philadelphia, Pa. with her two daughters and wonderful husband, Eric. She is entering her third year of medical school, with the goal of becoming an Emergency Medicine Physician. She enjoys spending time with her family and working on projects around the house.

WU, JUDITH

Judith Wu (Juju) is a first-time mom based in Orange, Calif. She has one child and hopes to have at least one more. She likes to go shopping when possible and loves going on vacations.

YOUNG, JENNIFER

Jennifer Young lives in Bethesda, Md. with her two children and husband, John. She likes finger-painting, playing on the jungle gym and dressing up like Cinderella (a good thing since these are the same activities her little ones enjoy).

ZARA, STEPHANIE

Stephanie Zara lives in Boonton Township, N.J. with her husband, George, and their daughter, Mary Alice, who is now a healthy 1-year-old, despite being born seven weeks premature. An artist, painter and photographer, she and her husband believe in attachment parenting, extended breastfeeding, delaying solids and that strong family bonds and a loving home are essential to a happy, healthy, loving family. They plan on having a large family and will homeschool their children.

ZIMMER, TIFFANY

Tiffany Zimmer lives in Towson, Md. with her daughter and husband, Mike. After having her daughter, she quit her full-time job in a public accounting firm to start her own practice, working out of her home. She enjoys spending time with her family, swimming, sewing and reading. Her favorite activity is going out on Saturday night dates with Mike when Gram (aren't moms great!) is available to babysit.